A Guide

to

Short Writing

Tasks

This book is dedicated to all those children who are studying with Heckingbottom Learning Ltd. for the 11+ - with me personally or using some of my on line resources. It is also dedicated to all those children that I have worked with in recent years – especially those who have provided examples of work for the book!

- Florrie McDaid
- Kimon Zannikos
- Niamh White
- Maxi Rowe
- Grace-Emily Childs
- Daisy Williams

And all the other children I've worked with this year. Some of the things we've done together have ended up in here!

Thank you!

For those of you who are using this book; hopefully, it will help you to get those one or two extra marks that will lift your score comfortably beyond the magic '303' that you are targeting.

Good luck to you all!

Table of Contents

Introduction

Writing is an essential part of our day to day education, and the emphasis is constantly on us as to how to improve our writing skills. It became a great concern in many of the Grammar schools, particularly here in the Essex area, that children were being groomed to get a place at a selective school by working on their VR skills and maths, with less emphasis on comprehension and very little work on writing skills. As a result, many children were getting into Grammar Schools who could barely produce a decent piece of written work and so were struggling to cope in many of their lessons once they got there.

Partly due to this, and partly due to other external factors, over the last few years, the CSSE (Essex) has asked students taking their exam to produce 2 short pieces of writing during the hour set aside for English. Their guidance is that each of these pieces of writing should take around 10 minutes to produce. These are marked together and an overall mark out of 15 is given; however, in the last couple of years, it has been fairly obvious that the writing questions are quite heavily weighted in the Essex 11+.

So far, these pieces of writing have focussed on just 2 key genres – descriptive writing and instructional writing; however, there can be no guarantee that they will stick to this and so it is a good idea to try a few other genres of writing as well. Many of the mock exams that you may sit in this area of the country will get you to try some of the other genres, just to keep you on your toes!

This booklet follows the methods that I have used to develop quick creative writing skills with the children I have worked with for a number of years – very successfully.

Children preparing for the 11+ in other areas or for Independent Schools may also have to produce some form of creative writing, and this booklet will be useful for them, too.

Additionally, although creative writing is teacher assessed, the current SATs assessments ask Year 6 children to produce work in a variety of genres, some of which should be short pieces of writing. If your child's school is moderated, they will be looking for examples of their writing over a period of time and will be expecting to see a range of genres. This booklet will help with the preparation for these assessments.

This booklet includes key points to show the sort of thing that you should include in each of the main genres of short writing tasks, as well as examples to show you the sort of thing you could aim for. It reflects questions from previous 11+ and SATS papers and includes a list of possible writing tasks that you might like to use for extra practice.

I suggest that everyone working through this booklet should get themselves a writing notebook that they will enjoy working in – not a plain exercise book, as they are too boring; something eye-catching and exciting!

The models used in this book owe a lot to the Pie Corbett 'Talk for Writing' method, where one learns a text, uses a text and then adapts a text. Don't worry if your early writing in each genre closely mimics mine. It's a great way of learning the styles and genres! As you become more confident, you will adapt and change until you take ownership of the genre. On a recent course, I was given the example of a student who starts University with just one recipe – cheese on toast. For the first week or so, they make cheese on toast, religiously and without fail. After a week or so, they think "'How about if I were to add some ham to my cheese on toast?" They add it and enjoy the results – which gives them confidence to try adding a few tomatoes the next day. Before they know it, they have created a whole new dish! From there, they move on to try other things on toast – and then without the toast! Suddenly, they can cook!

The same is true of writing. Follow the models closely until you feel confident. Adapt the models. Change a few words – then more words. Add words of your own and adapt the model. Before you know it, you will be a writer!

So, from this we learn that it is important to read the examples, read the hints and advice; follow the teaching through; and, most importantly of all, practise! The more you practise each type of writing, the easier it will be! Don't be afraid to magpie words and ideas that you find in this book. Hopefully, they will help you to become an even better writer.

VCOP, Sentence Openers and QAAG

VCOP

In all writing, remember Variety in VCOP is important – But what's it all about?

Vocabulary

Use interesting, ambitious vocabulary wherever possible. Remember: if it's hard to spell, it's good to use! Don't forget a range of amazing adjectives and powerful verbs as well.

Make sure you use metaphors, similes, personification, alliteration etc. in descriptive writing. Can you get some onomatopoeia in there too?

Connectives

Use an interesting range of connectives – not just and, but, then.

Try: - although, whereas, since, whilst, however, because, so, moreover, nevertheless, furthermore etc.

Can you start one of your sentences with 'Although …'?

Don't forget connectives of time in instruction writing.

Openers

Make sure you start your piece of writing in an interesting way. You want to catch the attention of the reader (your audience) from the very beginning! Rhetorical questions can help here.

Try to vary the way you start each sentence in your writing. It's far too easy (and boring!) to start each one with the subject or a subject pronoun.

Try starting with a verb, an adverb or an adverbial clause

Could you start with a preposition or an adjective, or even the object?

Punctuation

Check the accuracy of your basic punctuation – full stops, commas and capital letters.

Make sure you have written at least 2 paragraphs; but don't necessarily leave a line between each one. Use indentation!

Try to use either a question mark or an exclamation mark

Additionally, try to use at least 3 of the following in each piece.

( )	...	-	" "	;	:	's	n't

Openers

It is vitally important to grab the attention of our readers from the moment they start to look at our work. So, how can we do this? The answer is obvious - by starting our writing in an unusual way, we will make them want to read it! When you've done that, you need to keep your reader's attention by keeping the writing lively and varying your sentence starts.

Try not to start with the subject or a subject pronoun every time. This is the most common way of starting a sentence and much of the writing your examiner or marker reads will start in this way.

Who did it ... what did they do?

I, She, They, The old lady, Mrs. James   etc.

Here are some alternative ideas (and examples!)

- o Start with a question – preferably a rhetorical question.
    - • How would you feel if you were to meet a lion? What would you think?
    - • What do you think is the most important thing about school? I'll tell you! In my opinion, it is ...
- o Start with an adverb or an adverbial phrase – how was the action done? Where did it happen? When did it happen?

- Quickly, the boy picked up his book and ran out of the room.
- Ponderously, the tortoise plodded down the garden, eying the luscious lettuce in the vegetable patch. Would he get there before he was spotted?

- Start with an action – preferably an 'ing' word –
  - Running down the hill, she fell over and landed face down in the mud!
  - Chasing its tail, the dog looked like a spinning top – or an unlit, spinning Catherine wheel!
  - Opening the wrapper carefully, I hear the gentle rustling before the aroma escapes, jumping up to bite me on the nose!
  - Squeezing through the tiniest of gaps, she urged herself ever onwards.

- Start with a preposition.
  - Behind the rock, far away from preying eyes, the tiny mouse sat and waited.
  - Near to where the children played, some strange creature was lurking in its lair; something half-human, half-animal. What could it be?

- Start with a connective
  - Although everyone knows that monkeys are mischievous, few people are aware of how naughty they can be.

- Whilst I love all types of fruit, I have to say that by far my favourite is the peach.
- Moreover …
- Nevertheless …
- On the other hand …
- As a result …

o Start with an adjective
  - Small, silver and shiny; the coin lay there, unclaimed.

o Start with the object, rather than the subject
  - The umbrella which he held in his arms was, perhaps, the only really normal thing about him.
  - The green hat perched precariously on his cheeky, green face made you want to laugh!

o Start with a comparative or superlative adjective.
  - Smaller than all the other fish in the pond, Goldie darted through the weeds.
  - More urgent than ever was his need to reach home – to reach his mother.
  - The greatest reason has to be …

o Start with a simile
  - Like a somnolent statue perched on his rock, this majestic beast opened his massive mouth to emit an indolent roar.

- Like a silver coin emerging from a black, velvet purse, the moon crept out to brighten the countryside.
- As quiet as a tiny mouse, Emma cautiously emerged from her hiding place. Had he gone? Had he really gone?

QAAG

Another great hint I picked up on a course somewhere is to try to QAAG in every piece of writing if you really want to engage your reader. Across your two 10 minute tasks, try to ensure you have one example of each element of QAAG somewhere.

QAAG stands for:

QUESTION: Usually rhetorical – this is a great way to grab your reader's attention – to make them think about what you are saying. It's a great introduction for instructions and a fantastic conclusion for descriptive writing. It is also an absolute non-negotiable in advert writing!

ADDRESS YOUR READER: - make them feel that you are writing this for them!

- Have you ever wondered...?
- Could you imagine ...?
- Close your eyes and picture this scene.
- Try combining this with ...
- Imagine these scrumptious flavours mingling on your spoon

ASIDE: (Often written in brackets or between other forms of parenthesis) – this adds a little extra detail to help the reader understand or to help them picture what you are talking about. In instructional writing, you can use it in the ingredients to say what you prefer to use.

GENERALISATION: This is an 'everyone knows' type of statement, which can challenge your reader.

- Everyone thinks they know how to ... but would you like to know the really best way to ...?

- Of course, no-one can resist the cheeky face of a ...

- Everyone loves to spend time on a quiet, peaceful beach, surrounded by ...

- All ten year olds know that the best sweets are ...

Descriptive Writing

Here are two examples of descriptive writing produced by ten year olds in June 2016. The first was written by a girl; the second, by a boy. Neither of them were confident writers when we started in October – but look at what they are producing just 8 months later!

My Violin

Brown in colour, my violin makes a winsome, engaging sound. Its beckon turns into a command, crescendoing into a thunderous roar; it gets ever louder! As my delicate bow rocks over taut strings, the music resonates from my beautiful instrument. The smell of the maple wood tickles my nostrils whilst its unique markings tell a mysterious tale. My treasured violin never leaves my side.

What better possession could anyone wish for?

Florrie McDaid (aged 10)

Lost

The vast, tall, wizened trees beside my head stand steadily, their verdant, crinkly leaves dancing in the strong winds. Tearful and worried, I dash around the colossal forest, trying my hardest to just glimpse part of my mother's blue jacket or my father's orange jumper but, when you're lost, nothing makes you cheerful. The empty feeling inside your stomach doesn't help either when all you can hear is silence beyond you and behind you.

An aroma of mud and dirt surrounds me, with a slight smell of smoke from a bonfire elsewhere.

Would you like to be lost in the woods and feel this horrid sensation?

Maxi Rowe (aged 10)

So what makes a good piece of descriptive writing? It should:

- Drag its reader in from the first sentence

- Refer to around 3 of the 5 senses

- Use fantastic adjectives, great adjectival phrases and expanded noun-phrases.

  HINT: For at least 3 of your nouns, see if you can give at least 2 adjectives - one WOW word and one synonym, for it.

  Can you get three or four adjectives into your opening sentence?

- Use metaphors, similes, personification and/or alliteration.

- Ends in a way that attracts the reader's attention as well.

  A really good way to end is with a rhetorical question such as: 'Could you imagine a (noun) as/more (adjective) as this? Could you picture a (noun) as (adjective) as this?

Example: Peach Melba

One fruit that I can never resist is a succulently juicy, ripe, fragrant peach. The texture of its gently furry coat against my tongue; the gentle, inviting aroma calling my name and urging me to eat it; the vibrancy of flavour as I bite into it ... all of this makes the peach one of my all-time favourite fruits. However, to make your peach even more special, try mixing it with the sharpness of raspberries and rich, creamy ice cream in the form of a Peach Melba. Just one bite, one small taste, and every sense will be convinced.

Picture this scrumptious combination on a spoon, heading towards your mouth. Could you imagine a desert more appetising than this one?

OK, I hear you say. So how do I go about producing a piece of work as good as one of those I have just read?

Here is a quick series of lessons to help you.

Section 1 – Describing animals

Lesson 1 (20 to 30 minutes)

Let's start with the idea of an elephant.

Picture an elephant in front of you. You can even draw one if you like!

Before I give you any more hints, I would like you take 10 minutes or so to write a short description of an elephant. 5 or 6 sentences will be enough. When you've done that, come back to this book and we'll look at how to improve it.

Done that?

Now check your work through.

- Does it make sense, or have you missed out some words?

- Have you used full stops and capital letters appropriately?

- What other punctuation have you used?

- Underline all your adjectives. How many are there? Which is the best adjective on your page? Have you given most of your nouns an adjective or two to make them more powerful?

- Read through your verbs. Have you used strong verbs? Could you use better ones?

- How many times have you written the word 'elephant'? Once is ideal; twice is acceptable; more than that is excessive and repetitive – a smelly foot! Can you change any of these to alternative nouns or pronouns?

- Have you any other 'smelly feet' (words that are being repeated frequently)? Can you change them?

  Don't repeat smelly feet!

<u>Lesson 2</u> (45 minutes)

We're going to go back to our idea of an elephant, but this time we're going to look at it a different way.

- Go to the computer and open your favourite search engine.

- Pull up images of an elephant and look at them carefully. Look at the colour (are they really grey, or are they more of a muddy, browny-grey colour??), the shape and size of the features, the position.

- Choose your favourite image and print it off – preferably in the middle of an empty sheet of paper.

- Is it an African elephant or an Indian elephant? How can you tell (Shape and size of ears is a good give-away! Unlike his cousin, the African elephant has huge ears, the shape of the continent that he roams.)

- Draw arrows to some of the key features and write down any words or phrases that come to mind – what do the ears remind you of? Like giant fans? Great – we've got a simile! What is the trunk like? Can you find another simile?

- Now see if you can find a video of an elephant – there are hundreds on the net.

- Watch the way it moves; listen to the noise it makes as it roars, or trumpets. As you do so, make notes on your piece of paper.

- Jot down verbs, adjectives, nouns as they come to mind. Watch a couple of videos and make as many notes as you can. Don't worry if you write too many notes! You will only choose the best ideas.

- Use your thesaurus – can you improve on any of the words that you have chosen?

- Think about what you know about elephants.
    - Long living beasts
    - Live in herds
    - Main adult – female – is called the matriarch
    - Largest land mammal
    - Herbivore – spends most of the day eating!
    - Gentle giant

  Whilst we don't want a scientific account, one or two of these words can be used in your description.

- Now, read through your notes and underline all the really good words that you have put in there. Cross out anything you don't like – these are only notes, remember! (I usually ask my pupils to hold onto their notes – when we go through and mark the work together, we sometimes pull out bits that we could have used to extend sentences!)

- Think about how you could start your writing. Try not to start with the words 'An elephant …'. Could you start with one of your verbs? Could you get one of your metaphors or similes into your first clause?

<u>E.g.</u>

Raising her huge snake-like trunk, the matriarch trumpets a warning out to the rest of the herd. (verb, simile and implied metaphor)

Prowling through the jungle on its huge, tree-trunk legs, the massive elephant … (verb and metaphor)

Fanning its massive ears, this mighty beast … (verb and implied metaphor)

- Ending your writing is just as important as starting it.

Can you add a conclusory sentence, using the structure below? It will really enhance your writing if you can!

One ending style that I encourage my pupils to use is the rhetorical question below, filling in your own nouns and adjectives:

Could you imagine a (noun) as (adjective) as this?

E.g. Could you imagine an animal as majestic as this?

   Could you imagine a beast more powerful than this?

Can you picture a creature as magnificent as this one?

Now spend around 10 to 15 minutes writing your new description of an elephant. Read it through carefully. Does it make sense?

Check all the things I got you to look at in the previous lesson.

Compare the two pieces of writing – hopefully, you can see an improvement already!

Is there anything you still feel unhappy about? How could you change it?

<u>Lesson 3</u> (30 to 40 minutes)

This time, we're going to focus on a lion – the king of the Savannah – rather than an elephant for our description, but we are going to use the same method as in the previous lesson. Think about what you know about lions as well – it will help you

- Go to the computer and open your favourite search engine.

- Pull up images of a lion and look at them carefully. Look at the colour, the shape and size of the features, the position. What colours can you see? Where are the lions? Which positions do you like?

  Personally, my favourite picture shows a male lion asleep by a large rock. I can get a lot of ideas from that – including an amazing sentence start!

- Choose your favourite image and print it off – preferably in the middle of an empty sheet of paper.

- Draw arrows to some of the key features and write down any words or phrases that come to mind – particularly adjectives.

  Can you find a simile or a metaphor?

  Perhaps for the look of the lion – a somnolent, sleeping statue – or his mane (a fluffy wig/scarf)

- Now see if you can find a video of a lion – there are hundreds on the net.

- Watch the way it moves; listen to the noise it makes as it roars. As you do so, make notes on your piece of paper.

- Jot down verbs, adjectives, nouns as they come to mind. Watch a couple of videos and make as many notes as you can. Don't worry if you write too many notes! You will only choose the best ideas.

- Use a thesaurus and look up synonyms for some of the key words. What are the most powerful words that you can find?

- Think about what you know about lions and write down one or two facts.
  Remember: whilst we don't want a scientific account, one or two of these words can be used in your description.

- Now, read through your notes and underline all the really good words that you have put in there. Cross out anything you don't like – these are only notes, remember! (I usually ask my pupils to hold onto their notes – when we go through and mark the work together, we sometimes pull out bits that we could have used to extend sentences!)

- Think about how you could start your writing. Try not to start with the words 'A lion ...'. Could you start with one of your verbs or one of your similes? What else could you think of to start with?

  Here is my opening sentence:

  Like a somnolent statue perched on a gigantic rock, this majestic creature opens his enormous mouth and gives an indolent roar – but don't be fooled!

  What can you come up with?

- Don't forget your conclusory sentence: Could you imagine/picture a (noun – not lion) as (adjective) as this?

Lessons 4 – 7 (or more, if you wish!)

Following the above plans, try writing descriptions of a range of other animals – both wild and tame. Be as precise as you can – what specific animal are you looking at?

Some good ones include:

- Zebra

- Giraffe

- Hippopotamus

- Great White Shark

- Squirrel

- Cow

- Rabbit

- Dolphin

- Goldfish

I'm sure you can think of some others of your own.

Section 2 – Describing Food

Lesson 8

This is the one my pupils always enjoy, as it requires you to eat a sweet!

Go and get a chocolate bar of your choice. (I usually use a mini-fudge or an individual Twix for this lesson) Don't open it yet!

You will also need the following: coloured pens – at least 3 colours; A4 plain paper; pencil; your writing notebook.

- Draw a quick picture of it in the middle of a page of A4 paper (landscape), leaving loads of room around it.

- Draw 5 lines, evenly spaced, coming out of your image and write one of each of your 5 senses on the lines.

- Choose one of your coloured pens. Now, look at your chosen sweet.

  o What colours can you see? Write it by the 'sight' line.

  o What is it doing? (Personification is really easy in food description!) Is it beckoning you, calling to you, calling your name, shouting at you? Write this by the 'hearing' line.

You should now be able to create a fantastic opening sentence! Here is mine:

As I gaze down at the colourful, orange and purple wrapper, the sweet beckons to me, nagging at me and whispering my name.

- Now change your colour of pen and unwrap your sweet.

    o What can you hear? Jot down your ideas.

    o What does the sweet look like? Mine looks like a short, brown twig, covered in ridges of bark!

    o What does it smell like? Can you use the word 'aroma' in this? Can you add some personification (The sweet, chocolatey aroma jumped out and bit me on the nose.)

    o Touch the chocolate – what does it feel like?

- Jot down your ideas on your mind map.

At this point, you should be able to create 1 or 2 more sentences in your description. Remember to try and start each sentence in a different way. Here's mine:

"Opening the wrapper carefully, I hear the gentle rustling before the aroma escapes, jumping up to bite me on the nose! Excitedly, I run my fingers across the chocolate, feeling its coolness and the smooth yet bumpy texture, like the bark on a tree."

- Now change your pen colour again. Here comes the fun part!
- Bite into it (or break a bit off and put it in your mouth)
  - What did you hear?
  - What is the flavour like?
  - What is the texture like in your mouth? (That goes in the 'touch' section. Remember, it's not just your fingers that you touch things with! Your tongue has a lot of touch sensors in it!)
- Take another bite and see if you can make any more notes.

Now you have two things to finish off – the sweet and the description – and it's up to you which order you do it in!

Don't forget your conclusory sentence – Who could imagine a (noun) as (adjective) as this?

Description of a Fudge Bar

As I gaze at the azure writing on the bright, orange background, the packaging catches my attention. I rip open the wrapper to reveal a world of pure deliciousness. The beatific aroma invades my nostrils; the temptation's killing me. Chomping into the luxurious heaven, it orders me to eat more. The call gets ever louder. I can hear my stomach sigh in relief.

Who wouldn't want a snack as ambrosial as this?

Florrie McDaid (aged 10)

Lesson 9

This time, we are going to repeat the process of the previous lesson, but using a healthier option - a banana!

Go and get a banana. Don't open it yet!

You will also need the following: coloured pens – at least 3 colours; A4 plain paper; pencil; your writing notebook.

- Draw a quick picture of it in the middle of a page of A4 paper (landscape), leaving loads of room around it.

- Draw 5 lines, evenly spaced, coming out of your image and write one of each of your 5 senses on the lines.

- Choose one of your coloured pens. Now, look at your banana.

    o What colours can you see? Write it by the 'sight' line. What does it look like? What other shades and colours can you see other than yellow?

    o What is it doing? (Personification is really easy in food description!) Is it beckoning you, calling to you, calling your name, shouting at you? Write this by the 'hearing' line.

You should now be able to create a fantastic opening sentence! Use a similar structure to the one you produced for the sweet.

Now change your colour of pen and unwrap your sweet.

- o What can you hear? Jot down your ideas.

- o What does the banana look like? Think about shape and colour – is it really all cream? What shades can you see in it?

- o What does it smell like? Can you use the word 'aroma' in this? Can you add some personification again?

- o Touch the fruit – what does it feel like?

- Jot down your ideas on your mind map.

At this point, you should be able to create 1 or 2 more sentences in your description. Remember to try and start each sentence in a different way.

- Now change your pen colour again. Here comes the fun part!

- Bite into it (or break a bit off and put it in your mouth)

    - o What did you hear?

    - o What is the flavour like?

- What is the texture like in your mouth? (That goes in the 'touch' section, remember!)
- What can you see in the remaining banana? Can you see the seeds inside? What do they look like?

- Take another bite and see if you can make any more notes.

Now you have two things to finish off – the banana and the description – and it's up to you which order you do it in!

Don't forget your conclusory sentence – Who could imagine a (noun) as (adjective) as this?

Lessons 10 to 13 (or further!)

Use the same method to describe a range of other foods (including sweets).

Some really good ones are:

- Apples
- Strawberries or other berries
- Fruit salad
- Lasagne
- Shepherds' pie or cottage pie
- Paella
- Fish and chips
- Ice cream

- Ice cream sundae

- Sticky toffee pudding

- Apple crumble

- A favourite drink

... but you may like to think of others yourself

Ice Cream Sundae

As cold as the arctic, as colourful as the rainbow, the ice-cream stares with glaring, sprinkle eyes. Its cone is as decorative as a Roman tapestry. It has kaleidoscopic and vibrant colours, including: pale pink, creamy white, lemon yellow and many, many more. Its smell is a creamy wonderland; its feel is a spongy pillow; it tastes like an icy dream, making my taste buds tingle with happiness! This ice-cream is as loquacious as I am, whispering gently, "Eat me; eat me!"

Who could resist a sweet treat as luxurious as this?

Grace-Emily Childs (aged 10)

Section 3 – Describing places or scenes

Now you are beginning to feel more confident about descriptive writing, try widening the theme.

A busy place

Think of a place that you know such as a shopping mall, a fairground, a football stadium, an airport etc. Try writing one detailed sentence to answer each of these questions. Link them carefully and you should have a good description.

- Where are you? Why are you there? Why is it so busy?

- What can you see around you? Think about looking in all directions.

- What can you hear? Try to give more than one thing. Can you give an idea of the clamour (din) coming from all around?

- What aromas can you smell – pleasant or unpleasant!

- What does it feel like? Why does it feel like this?

- How do you feel? Happy, nervous, frightened, overwhelmed etc. – why?

- Give a good conclusory sentence using the structure I have been showing you. Who could imagine a (noun) as (adjective) as this?

Lost

When I was lost, I felt isolated and abandoned; like I was loved no more, hated.

Wherever I looked, there were crowds of people. There was a clown, babies, doctors and families. Everyone was there, except for my mum. She was nowhere. It sounded as if Mum was calling me calling my name; but no matter which direction I looked, she was not there. A tear trickled down my cheek. Had she run away from me? Did my mum not love me anymore?

I had to find her!

Niamh White (aged 10)

<u>A quiet place</u>

Think of a place that you know such as a park, a beach, a spot in the garden, a place by a river or stream etc. Try writing one detailed sentence to answer each of these questions. Link them carefully and you should have a good description.

- Where are you? Why are you there? Why is it so quiet?

- What can you see around you? Think about looking in all directions.

- What can you hear? Try to give more than one thing. Can you give an idea of the peacefulness coming from all around? (I had one child telling me that it was so quiet, she could hear the flowers whispering their secrets to one another!)

- What aromas can you smell – pleasant or unpleasant!

- What does it feel like? Why does it feel like this?

- How do you feel? Why?

- Give a good conclusory sentence using the structure I have been showing you. Who could imagine a (noun) as (adjective) as this?

Task: Describe a tree. It can be real; or one from your imagination; but make your description vivid.

Imagine a tree where the trunk is a giant candy cane; where the branches are made out of Twix bars; where the leaves are marshmallows filled with Skittles, M&Ms and Smarties and the marshmallow leaves are coated in fizzy sherbet. In Candy Land, there is such a thing.

This tree is planted on an island made out of chocolates. With its candy cane trunk coated in white chocolate, it is by far the most delicious tree on earth. This amazing creation is called The Tooty-Licious Tree.

Could you imagine a more appetising tree?

Niamh White (aged 10)

Section 4 - Describing People

As in all descriptions, it is essential to describe more than one element of the person. Don't just focus on what they look like – talk about the personality as well. Refer to more than one sense and use as many great adjectives as you can to help your writing.

Think carefully: what is this person like?

- Look at a character on the outside: – short, tall, freckled, tanned, pale skin, pallid, hair colour, eye colour, pretty, ugly, plain etc.

- Look at a character on the inside: - brave, valiant, devious, sneaky, ingenious, intelligent, smart, cunning, artful, caring, honest, fair, just, unjust, dishonest etc.

- What do they sound like?

  o Her voice was as calming as a gentle stream

  o His tinny voice grated against my senses.

  o His voice was an explosion of thunder, rattling the doors

- Smell – this could be literal – the fragrance of the perfume they wear – or metaphorical.

  o Does Grandma's kind voice smell of roses, perfume and patience?

- What other characteristics can you turn into a smell? Try anger, love, etc.

My description of Mr Tumnus, the Faun. (with apologies to CS Lewis!)

The person facing me was only a little taller than I was; however, the umbrella which he held in his right arm (keeping off the rapidly falling snow) was, perhaps, the only really normal thing about him. From the waist upwards, he resembled a man – but below this, everything seemed strange! His legs were shaped like those of a goat, covered in glossy, black fur, and he also had the feet of a goat – no shoes needed! He also had a tail, which I took some time to notice, as it was caught over the arm that was holding the umbrella, so as to keep it from trailing in the snow.

Around his neck, he wore a red, woollen scarf, and his skin had a reddish hue too. His face was friendly and pleasant, although it seemed a little strange in many ways. He had a short, pointed beard and curly hair – out of which grew two horns, one on each side of his forehead. The smile on his face was calming and welcoming, not at all frightening, and his voice, when he spoke, had a wonderfully melodic quality.

"I knew you would come!" he told me. "I was waiting for you! Won't you come with me and meet the family?"

Could you resist a creature as amazing as this? I certainly couldn't …!

More ideas for themes for Descriptive Writing

This list is also repeated at the back of the book, as you will probably be keen to get onto the next section by now!

Remember - It often helps to find a picture on the internet to help you with your descriptions!

Write 6 or 7 well-structured sentences to describe:

- Your favourite animal
- A cat or a dog
- A tree in a particular season (or try 4 pieces, each one reflecting one of the 4 seasons!)
- A tree from your imagination
- Your best friend
- A relative of yours that you admire
- A relative or person whom you dislike
- Your favourite teacher
- Your least favourite teacher! (A really fun one to do! – Just think of Professor Snape from the Harry Potter books to see how well it can be done!)
- Your ideal bedroom
- Your most precious possession
- Your favourite fruit
- Your favourite meal

- Your favourite food item

- A hot dessert

- A hot desert! (Make sure you know which is which!)

- Your favourite drink

- Your favourite ice-cream

- A vehicle you like (or want to own when you're old enough!)

- Someone's job – be careful to describe!

- An unusual house – there are some lovely ones on Google Images to give you some ideas

- Your favourite place

- A forest

- An orchard

- A flower – from your imagination or one that you can actually see.

- A haunted house

- An alien lands in your garden. Can you describe him?

- Can you describe his spaceship?

- You are standing, facing an unusual door. In 6 or 7 sentences, describe it and describe your feelings as you prepare to open it.

- The door creeks open and you walk in. In 6 or 7 sentences, describe what you can see and how you feel as you walk in.

- You have just walked through a portal into a mysterious new land. In 6 or 7 sentences, describe what is in front of you.

- Imagine you are lost. Write a description to show what you can see and how you feel.

Instructional Writing

Before going any further, try what we call a 'cold task' and write a set of instructions to show me how to make a sandwich with just one, preferred filling.

Don't worry about it - just write it the way you've been taught, or the way you think you should write it. I'll show you how to make it better over the next few pages.

Now read your instructions through and check:

- Have you punctuated accurately – especially full stops and capital letters?

- Have you written an introduction?

- Have you listed what you will need?

- Have you listed the steps in the correct order?

- Have you added any extra detail, or have you just told me the basic steps?

- Have you done anything to catch the reader's eye and make them want to read it?

So what turns good instructions into great instructions?

Great instructional writing should:

- Clearly state what their purpose is.

- Where appropriate, list what is needed to complete the task. (This is a great way to ensure that you have used colons and semi-colons.)

- Have a clear list of instructions in their correct chronological order, each of which should be clearly numbered.

- Use ordinal conjunctions such as 'First', 'Next', 'After that' etc.

- Each instruction should be clear, compact and easy to understand.

- Detail should be added to add interest and to catch the reader's attention.

<u>Example:</u>

<u>How to write instructions.</u>

Of course, everyone thinks they know how to write instructions, but have you ever wondered how to write the best instructions it is possible to write? Follow this guide, and you can't go wrong!

To create great instructional writing, you will need the following: something to write on; something to write with; and your (hopefully intelligent) brain!

1. First of all, always start with an introduction to catch the reader's eye. A rhetorical question followed by a simple statement is a great way to start. I've also used a generalisation here!

2. Make sure you know what equipment or ingredients are needed to complete the task. If you can make a detailed list, with an aside (in brackets) or with adjectives, then you can use semi-colons to separate out the different items – bonus points for punctuation!

3. Next, ensure that you know the correct order for the main part of the instructions. Try not to have more than 5 steps for a ten minute task so as not to run out of room (or space)

4. Put the number 1 at the extreme left hand side of the paper and carefully start your instructional writing, beginning with the first step. Start with an ordinal conjunction such as 'First,'

5. When you have written that instruction, move to the next line and write the number 2 at the extreme left hand side. Write the next step of the instructions, beginning with a different ordinal conjunction such as 'Next,' or 'After that,' making sure that you follow each of your ordinal conjunctions with a comma. Remember: you can use more than one sentence for each step!

6. Continue until you have written all the steps down, starting at least 3 of your steps with ordinal conjunctions or fronted adverbials.

7. Finish with a simple conclusory statement – perhaps a sentence of advice or a suggestion to relax and enjoy your success!

Remember, when you are writing instructions, it is essential not to panic, as this could cause you to miss a step. It is equally important not to 'waffle' too much, as your reader will lose track of the processes involved and will not be able to follow your instructions!

Now, let's put that into practice by thinking about how you could improve your instructions for making your sandwich.

The first thing you need to do is to go and make your sandwich. Take a piece of paper with you as you do so, and make a note of all the ingredients (not equipment – this is only a 10 minute task!) that you use as well as the steps that you go through in the process.

Use a flow chart or sequence diagram to help you (see overleaf)

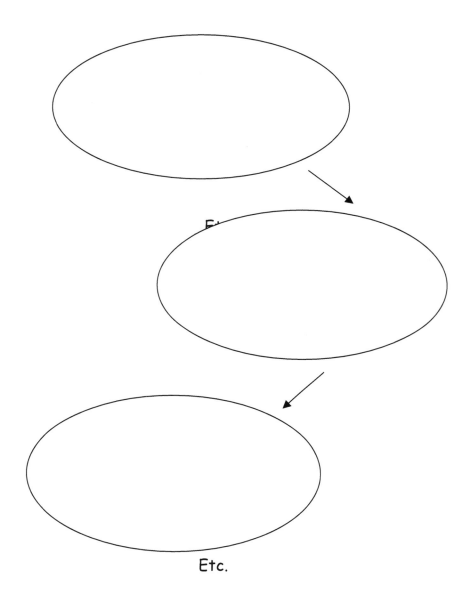

Etc.

Write your ingredients in the top box, then make a note of the stages that you go through.

Introduction

Every good piece of writing needs an introduction and instructions are no exception: however, with instructions, it' a great opportunity to use a generalisation, a question and a statement.

Structure:

> Everyone thinks they already know how to ... but do you know how to create the very best ... in the world? Follow these instructions and you will soon be confident!

Example:

> Everyone thinks they know how to make a sandwich, but do you know how to create the best ham and cucumber sandwiches in the world? Follow these instructions and you will soon be extremely confident!

Now, use two sentences and vaguely following the instructions above, see if you can create your introduction. Don't feel that you have to change too many words at this point.

Use the model – stick to it as much as you need to! As you feel more confident, you will be able to adapt it more and more, and that is great!

Equipment/Ingredients

This is a great opportunity to show that you know how to use colons and semi-colons – even if you don't think you're totally confident, they're easy to use here!

The colon (:) precedes the detailed list of items.

The semi-colon (;) separates out each item in a detailed list (rather than commas)

Structure

To create … you will need the following: item one with detail; item 2 (perhaps with an aside to state your personal preference); item three; and item four.

NOTICE: When we use semi-colons to separate out items in a detailed list, we even use one before the word 'and'. This means that you can actually use more than one 'and' in your list and people won't be confused!

Example:

To make a brilliant ham and cucumber sandwich, you will need the following: two slices of fresh wholemeal or granary bread; two slices of hand carved, roasted ham

(I prefer unsmoked, but others might have different preferences); 10 slices of cucumber; and soft, easy spread butter.

Now try your own version of this. Again, don't be afraid to stick closely to the model. As you become more confident, you will be able to adapt it more and more.

Try writing lists of ingredients/equipment for a variety of other instructions. It will soon seem like second nature!

Writing the actual instructions

Remember to think the steps through carefully so as to get them in chronological order. It helps to actually do the activity you are writing instructions for and to write them in a flow chart the first few times, which is why I got you to do that first. Make brief notes, with shorthand if you like, laying the precise order that you need.

Here are mine:

1. Butter bread – both slices – one side

2. Lay cuc - one layer – on bread

3. Cover - ham

4. Another layer of cuc

5. Cover with 2nd bread – butter down

6. Cut - 4 (diagonally) – eat.

Now write your own notes for your sandwich. Remember – these are notes; use abbreviations that you will understand. You will develop these in a minute!

Finally, you can transfer these notes into detailed instructions. Add more detail to your ideas – adjectives, more precision etc.

Make sure you use 'bossy verbs' – the imperative form, with minimal use of pronouns. You're telling them what to do, not making suggestions!

Example:

1. First, place your 2 slices of bread down on a clean working surface. Carefully butter one side of each slice, making sure that you have buttered the whole surface.

2. Next, cover one slice of bread with 5 slices of cucumber. I find that one slice in each corner and a

further one in the middle usually provides and even cover.

3. Now it's time for the ham! Place your delicious ham carefully over the cucumber, ensuring even coverage, then place the remaining slices of cucumber over the ham for an extra 'crunch' as you bite in.

4. Place the final slice of bread over the top of your ham and cucumber and cut it into 4, delicious pieces.

   N.B. This is the point when you decide how refined you want your sandwich to appear. If you are entertaining visitors (including grandparents) and want your sandwich to look really posh and impressive, remove the crusts first and then cut it diagonally, from corner to corner.

5. Finally, serve neatly laid out on a plate with a small handful of Walkers Ready Salted crisps for additional texture.

   Now relax and enjoy your scrumptious snack with a nice cup of tea or a delicious fizzy drink.

Lesson 2

Now that you have managed to create detailed instructions for making a sandwich, see if you can adapt it to create instructions for making cheese, beans or jam on toast.

Remember:

1. Make it first, and make notes as you do so.

2. Introduction – Everybody thinks they know how to ... but would you like to know how to make the best ...? Follow these instructions and...

3. Ingredients – detailed, with a colon to start and semi-colons to separate out the items.

   To make this delicious snack, you will need the following:

4. Detailed instructions in the right order – numbered, with ordinal conjunctions where appropriate.

5. A conclusory statement –

   Now relax and enjoy ... with ...

Here are some examples written by some of my pupils this year. You will notice a similarity in style but, as I try to remind them regularly, it is unlikely that more than 2 or 3 of you will be marked by the same person!

How to get dressed to go out on a snowy day

Do you want to know how to fully prepare yourself for a snowy day? Well, follow these instructions and you can't go wrong.

You will need the following: a hat; gloves; a scarf; 2 pairs of socks; a t-shirt; a jumper; a coat; some wellies; and underwear.

1. Firstly, take your t-shirt and jumper. Put on your t-shirt followed by your jumper

2. Next, take your underwear, leggings and trousers. Put your underwear in first, followed by your leggings and then your trousers.

3. After you have put on your bottom half clothes, take your two pairs of socks. Thinner pair first, then the woolly pair

4. Now, wrap your scarf around your neck, hat on your head and fluffy gloves on your hands. Finally, pull your wellies on your feet and your coat on top.

Did you ever think you could feel so warm on a winter's day?

You are now as snug as a bug in a rug!

By Daisy Williams (Aged 10)

How to make a cup of tea

Have you ever wondered how to make a tea that everyone will want to drink? Well, follow this guide and you can't fail!

You will need the following: a tea bag to make the tea with; a mug to put the tea in; running water to boil; a kettle to boil the water in; and some milk.

1. Start by pouring some water into a kettle (about 500 ml) and then turn it on.

2. When it's finished boiling, place a teabag of your choice into a mug, then pour the boiled water on top.

3. Finally, if you have chosen English Breakfast Tea, you should add a tablespoon of milk

4. Stir for a while. Now that you have created your masterpiece, sit back, relax and enjoy.

Kimon Zannikos (aged 10)

How to make a hot drink

Have you ever wondered how to make the best hot chocolate drink ever? Follow this guide and it can't go wrong.

To do this, you will need the following: your favourite mug, cocoa powder, a kettle available and a tap.

1. Firstly, tip approximately two teaspoons of cocoa powder into the mug you have chosen.

2. Next, boil the kettle, making sure that you have enough water in it.

3. Then, when you have boiled your water, pour it over the cocoa powder, keeping cautious about burning yourself.

4. Penultimately, add some milk to cool your drink down a bit.

5. Finally, you can do the best part: drink it!

Good luck and enjoy!

Florrie McDaid (aged 10)

Now that you are beginning to get the hang of instruction writing, it is time to have a go at more of these of your own.

Remember the format:

Introduction – generalisation, question, statement

In order to (do this) you will need the following: detailed list separated by semi-colons

Instruction – detailed in 4 or 5 numbered steps, preferably with fronted adverbials or ordinal conjunctions.

Quick conclusion

Here are some ideas for Instructional Writing

Again, many of these are repeated at the end of the book, so don't feel you have to do them all now!

In 6 or 7 sentences, give clear instructions as to how to:

- Make cheese on toast
- Make jam on toast
- Make a sandwich
- Make a hot drink
- Make an ice cream sundae
- Make a birthday card for a friend
- Wrap a present
- Wash your hands

- Brush your teeth
- Wash your hair
- Have a shower
- Bathe a pet
- Feed a pet
- Get dressed for school
- Get an alien/Stone-age child ready for school so they will fit in
- Get changed for PE
- Prepare to do some painting
- Prepare for an art lesson
- Brush your teeth
- Clean your shoes
- Put on your socks and shoes
- Play your favourite playground game
- Play your favourite board game
- Play a card game of your choice
- Tidy your bedroom in 5 minutes (think outside the box here!)
- Put a magic spell on your teacher/tutor

<u>Other genres,</u>

These are not currently used in the Essex 11+ but are, nevertheless, worth practising for SATs and for any other 11+ exams that you may need to take – to independent schools or to schools outside this immediate area.

Writing Conversations

There are several essential things to watch out for here but, above all, make sure you know how to punctuate speech!

- Use 2 characters and ensure that each one says at least 2 things in order to create a conversation.

- Introduce the conversation briefly.] in an interesting way- try to pull the reader in.

- Make sure you open and close each section of speech appropriately. You do NOT have to use '66 and 99.' (Personally, I hate those – they are clumsy, awkward and often over-sized!) Simple speech marks, like the ones you see in your reading books or on the computer, are fine.

- Punctuation such as commas, exclamation marks and question marks should usually be <u>inside</u> the closing speech marks.

- Remember the comma, comma rule for interrupted direct speech.

  "Don't forget," Mum whispered as she switched off the late closed the bedroom door, "when you wake up, it'll be your birthday!"

- New speaker, new line; same speaker, same line.

- If you are addressing someone in direct speech, separate out their name from the rest of what is being said with a comma.

  E.g. "Right now means right now, David!" his mum shouted.

- Try to avid use of the word 'said'. Although many famous authors over-use it, you need to be using this opportunity to 'show off'. How many alternatives can you use in a 10 minute writing task?

- Use an adverbial phrase for at least one part of your conversation to show how it is being said or to show what the person is doing as they say it. Can you use a fronted adverbial, or use it as an embedded clause?

Example: Bedtime!

What's bedtime like in your house? Well, in ours it's always pretty chaotic. Here is a typical night with my little brother!

"It's half past eight; bedtime, David," Mum remarked, looking up from her book at her son, who was busily playing on his X-box with his father.

"Oh, Mum, 5 more minutes, please!" David responded, without looking up. "I'm about to win and I'm nearly at an all-time highest score!"

"That's what you say every night!" Dad chuckled, manipulating his player further along the course. "You need a good night's sleep if you're going to get those high grades!"

"You just don't want to lose!" David retorted.

"True," replied Dad, "but then again, nor do you!"

"If you're not up those stairs 10 minutes from now, I'm turning the TV off at the mains and hiding the X-box controls for the next month!" Mum laughed. "Honestly, you two – you're as bad as one another!"

Aren't you glad you don't live in a house as manic as ours?

Example: Hunger!

Two enormous lions, brothers, both with manes like matted hearth rugs, were prowling across the savannah, roaring loudly as proof of their dominance.

"I'm starting to feel a bit peckish," Leo growled, scanning the horizon for tasty prey.

"Peckish!" Simba replied with a menacing roar. "You're only peckish? I'm starving! The next zebra's definitely mine! Totally and completely!"

"Hmm. We'll see about that!" Leo started to creep towards a nearby oasis.

"Have you seen something?" his friend queried.

"Wait and see!" came the reply. "If so, I might let you have a share!"

Who will consume the larger portion of the prey?

Now you are getting the hang of this genre, it is time to have a go at a few conversations of your own. Try some of these – or use ideas of your own.

- Write a conversation between you and one of your parents, where you are requesting 10 more minutes before bedtime.
- Write a conversation between you and a friend, where you are arranging to go to the cinema at the weekend.
- Write a conversation between 2 cows in a field
- Write a conversation between 2 goldfish in a bowl.
- Write a conversation between 2 dogs in a park.
- Imagine a tree or a lamp post reacting to a dog who is about to use it as a toilet. Write their conversation.
- Write a conversation between the Wolf and one of the 3 Little Pigs.
- Write a conversation between 2 of the Godmothers of Sleeping Beauty at some stage in the story.
- Write a conversation between 2 characters from different books by the same author.
- Write a conversation between an author and a character from their book – for example, one of the unpleasant children in Charlie and the Chocolate Factory challenging Roald Dahl about their 'punishment'.

Play Scripts

Whilst these are similar to conversations, there are also different things to remember.

- Introduce your play script by setting the scene in a simple way, answering three key questions: Who is in the scene; where are they; and what are they doing?

- Give stage directions to show what the actors should do. In real plays, these are show in italics, but you could just use brackets

- Start by naming the speaker and follow this with a colon every time to separate the speaker from what is being said.

- Do NOT use speech marks for the speech!

- Speech should start in a similar place horizontally. On a computer, we can use the tab bar to ensure this.

- Use stage directions (in brackets after the colon) to show how things are being said.

Example

Cast: Two tramps, Mel and Sid

It is a dark, cold night. Mel and Sid are sitting on a green park bench, wrapped in blankets and other materials. The street lights are dim and the sound of the traffic can just be heard in the background.

Mel: (Shivering and hugging himself to keep warm) Ooh, it's so cold out here, do you think it might rain?

Sid: (Shrugs his shoulders) Dunno.

Mel: Not very talkative tonight are you? What's up?

Sid: (Huffs a bit and stretches his legs out) Dunno.

Mel: I was thinking about my holiday, (looks up to the sky) all that sun and luxury.

Sid: (Glumly) Dunno what for; it ain't ever gonna 'appen.

Mel: (waving a pink ticket in the air) You never know – look what I found tonight!

Sid: (Brightens and makes a grab for it!) When's it drawn?

Mel: (smirking) Tonight!!! Shall we go watch?

(The two tramps depart to watch the draw at the local 24 hour supermarket)

Example 2: Hey Diddle, Diddle

Cast: Cat, Cow, Little Dog, Dish, Spoon.

Scene 1

The Cat stands alone in a large, empty space, playing the fiddle badly. We hear the mangled strains of Hey, diddle, diddle in the background.

Cat: (Proudly) I am so good at the fiddle. Nobody can fiddle as well as me! I am the best fiddler in town!

(Enter Cow)

Cow: Oh, hi, Cat. How are you?

Cat: Yeah, good thanks. Just brushing up on my music skills. Great, aren't I?

Cow: (turning up his nose.) For a cat, I suppose!

Cat: (drops the fiddle and crosses his arms in anger.) How dare you! If you're so good, why don't you do something amazing like … (thinking hard) like … like … (suddenly thinks of it) jump over the moon!

(Enter Little Dog with a moon on a stick)

Cow: Easy! I can do that with my eyes shut! (Turns, takes a run up, jumps and flies straight over the moon – which could be held on a stick by

Little Dog. Cow turns to pull a face at Cat,
then exits, stage right.)

Cat: Show off!

Little Dog: (Laughing.) You're so funny! You two argue like
        a married couple!

(Cat storms off stage, stage right, carrying fiddle. Enter
Dish and Spoon carrying suitcases!)

Little Dog: Oh, hello, Spoon. Hello, Dish! You just missed
        a cracker! Cat and Cow were at it again!
        Made me laugh so much, my sides split (turns
        to reveal a split in his costume)

Dish: Well, that's great – but we can't talk now.
        We're in a bit of a hurry! Can't stop! (Looks
        around nervously)

Spoon: (looking around, equally nervously.) Yes, yes!
        Must hurry!

Dog: You two aren't running away with together are
        you? OMG! Must tell Cat and Cow! They'll
        never believe it!

(All exit – Dish and Spoon - Stage left; Little Dog – Stage
        Right)

Now that you are getting the idea of this genre, have a go at some of these and see what you think:

- It's bedtime and you don't want to go to bed yet. Write the play script!

- Write a play script showing a child who does not want to do their homework and the parent who is insistent that they do!

- Turn one of your conversations into a play script (Remember to set the scene and give stage directions!)

- I turned 'Hey Diddle Diddle' into a play script. Take a different Nursery Rhyme and turn it into a play script.

- Write a short scene from a well-known Fairy Tale as a play script. Can you add a twist to it?

- Read a couple of paragraphs of a classic book, particularly a section with dialogue. Can you turn it into a play script?

Postcards

These are, basically, another form of descriptive writing – but they have an element of persuasion too, as you need to persuade me (the reader) that I would like to join you there!

- Unless they give you a proper postcard layout, all you need to write is the message part. You won't be expected to draw your own layout!

- Writing a postcard is like writing a short note. You don't have a lot of space, you may need to shorten what you are writing – e.g. instead of 'I'm having a great time' you might write 'Having a fantastic time!'

- Postcards are fairly informal – use abbreviations such as I've, I'm etc. but don't be tempted to use text speak!

- Postcards should begin with a date and a greeting

- Sets the scene – where are you? What is it like? What is the best thing about the place where you are staying?

- Describe something that you have done, working from experience – a trip to a waterpark is always a good one to choose.

- Express emotion! How do you feel? What are you enjoying? Why?

Example:

18.6.16

Dear Grannie and Grandad

Having an amazing time here in Torrevieja. The villa is fantastic, with a beautiful pool (which has been empty some of the time, believe it or not!) We've been to the local market – where the aromas of fruit and the sounds of the hawkers really engulfed my senses. Yesterday, Mum and Auntie Jane took us to the water park. Discombobulating or what? We zoomed down a range of slides. James and Peter went down a really steep slide, but I was too nervous! My favourite ride was one where you whooshed down in a giant rubber ring! Some bits were dark – really scary – and others were really fast!

Missing you – wish you were here too – but having a fantastic holiday at the same time.

Your ever-loving grand-daughter.

Imagine you are on holiday in France with some friends.

Ask yourself some questions to get your ideas going.

- How did you get there?
- What is the place you are staying in like?
- What is the weather like?
- What kind of things have you done or would like to do?
- Where did you visit?

Here are some words you might use in your message:

Apartment   hotel   airport   beach   pool
weather   tours   pub shopping   duty free   sight-
seeing   souvenirs   views   trips   swimming waterpark   slides   visited   Disneyland

Trip of a lifetime

Your parents have won the Lotto and you have all just gone on the trip of a lifetime.

Think about where in the world you might be. What experience would you really enjoy?

- Climbing a mountain in Nepal
- Skiing in Austria
- Shopping in New York
- Riding an elephant in India
- Walking along the Great Wall of China
- Watching a particular football match
- Visiting a particular country

Take time to think of your own ideas as well; then write a postcard to a friend describing this experience of a lifetime.

Can you write a postcard after a day spent …?

- In London
- At the Sea life Centre
- On your most recent holiday
- After a special event
- After visiting a water park
- After visiting a theme park
- Whilst staying with friends
- Write a postcard home in the role of a WW1 soldier from the trenches, or a Roman Soldier in Britain
- From a child who has just been evacuated in WW2
- After day out for the birthday of one of your siblings!
- From a character in one of your reading books.
- From a family holiday in another country
- From a School Journey (holiday) or other Camp

Diary Entries

Again, these are another form of descriptive writing.

Key Features:

- Date – when the events happened. You would usually write on the day it happened – today, earlier on, possibly last night

- First person – you writing about yourself

- Past tense – you are writing about what has happened

- Self-reflective – write about your feelings, thoughts, hopes and fears

- Rhetorical questions – ask questions about what is happening

- Asides – for your future self to look back on and understand!

- Different punctuation marks – used to emphasise your words

- Paragraphs – used when a new person, place, topic or time is introduced

How are they set out?

- Day by day or event by event

- Set out like a series of letters

- Start with 'Dear' So and So

- Mixture of events and feelings
- Can include doodles (not a good idea in an exam situation, though – they are just assessing the contents!)
- Includes informal, colloquial language, such as slang – 'I was like, OMG! How good are they?'
- Also includes more formal language and great descriptive vocabulary
- Uses great temporal conjunctions (time connectives) – subsequently, at last, initially, after a while, later on, eventually etc.
- Ends with a salutation – from, love from etc.

Example: A Good Day

Friday 30th November 2012

Dear Diary

I reckon I had the best day EVER today. When I woke up this morning, the sun was already shining through the curtains and I could smell breakfast cooking downstairs. I jumped out of my bed, threw on my school clothes and skipped down to the kitchen.

A delicious breakfast of pancakes with syrup was waiting for me on the table, so I gobbled it down as quick as a flash! Then, I grabbed my school bag, shouted "Bye!" to my mum and dashed out of the door to school.

When I arrived at school, my teacher handed my homework back to me and a huge grin spread across her face. Guess what? I got full marks on it! I couldn't believe it! We even had my favourite lessons in the morning (Maths and Geography).

Before I knew it, it was lunchtime. The menu today was my favourite: Spaghetti Bolognaise followed by Chocolate sponge pudding – yummy!

The afternoon flew by, and we ended the school day with a really fun game of Dodgeball. We all cheered when my team won (naturally!)

After school, I came home and was met with the most amazing surprise; my mum told me that we were going out to the cinema and to Pizza Hut for dinner. We had a fantastic time!

Right now, I'm sitting on my bed writing this, remembering all the fun things that have happened today. I hope tomorrow is just as good!

Jamie

Now that you are beginning to understand this genre, have a go at some of the following:

- Write a diary entry for a really great day out/ a horrible day out. Contrasting diary entries are good fun here too!

- Write a diary entry after a school trip

- Write a diary entry for your birthday

- Write a diary entry for your brother/sister's birthday. Think about what you might have been expected to do!

- Write a diary entry from the point of view of an inanimate (non-living) object such as a pencil, a paper clip, a pen, a toothbrush, a peg, your teddy bear or something you choose for yourself

- Write a diary entry from the point of view of a piece of food! Such as a Brussel sprout, a baked bean, a sausage.

- Write a diary entry for a soldier in WW1 or WW2

- Write a diary entry for a child who has just been evacuated in WW2

- Imagine you are Charlie Bucket. Write a diary entry for the day you found your golden ticket to Willie Wonka's Chocolate Factory.

- Write a diary entry for a character from one of your reading books

Persuasive Writing

<u>Remember to PEE in Persuasive Writing!</u>

We use persuasive writing to share our points of view with others – to get them to agree with us.

Persuasive writing appears all around us:

- Adverts
- Letters in the newspaper
- Shopping catalogues
- Posters and Billboards
- Holiday brochures
- Articles in magazines
- Trailers for films
- Fliers through your door

They all use a similar type of language – one that tries to encourage you to share their point of view.

Did you know ...?

In persuasive writing, it is important to PEE!

- Point – make your point clearly

- Elaborate – give a bit more detail to strengthen your argument

- Evidence and Examples

Be positive – tell everyone why you are right.

Give your point; then elaborate with more detail to justify your argument. Don't be afraid to add opinion – can you add some facts as well.

Example

Everyone knows that fruit is good for you, but did you know that kiwis are actually one of the best fruits you can eat? (Point) Not only are they delicious and easy to eat, but they are also packed with Vitamin C. (Elaborate) In fact, gram for gram, your delicious, ripe kiwi contains more Vitamin C than an orange (Example).

How would you persuade people to spend their money on …?

- Bananas

- Your special sandwich

- A new bike

- A yacht

- An ice cream

Persuasive Vocabulary

Here are some really useful words and phrases to use in persuasive writing.

- o I am writing to...

- o Is it really worth ...?

- o This needs to be dealt with...

- o All children agree that ...

- o A friend of mine says...

- o No-one but a complete idiot would believe that...

- o We can do without this...

- o When I asked my class, 75% of them agreed with me that ...

- o Of course...

- o It is disgraceful that...

- o How unfair!

- o Another thing...

- o I believe that...

- o How could we possibly... ?

- o I hope that you agree...

- On the other hand …

- Do you want to be part of… ?

- An intelligent person like yourself…

Persuasive Adverts

Adverts are the most common form of persuasive writing you'll find - on TV, on websites, in magazines, newspapers, leaflets and on notice boards. They are a special sort of persuasive writing. Their purpose is to sell a product or a service. They do this by aiming at a particular type of customer. They use carefully chosen, positive language. They appeal to some aspect of the reader's personality.

Think about the sort of words people use in adverts. Because people are trying to make their products sound good, you'll hear lots of positive, persuasive words such as:

- Great, fantastic, brilliant, marvellous, brilliant
- Free, special offer
- New, improved
- exclusive

People also use persuasive writing to convince you that their point of view on a subject is right, or that someone else's point of view is wrong.

- Adverts should always use bias. This means only putting forward one side of an argument; for example, only telling you the good things about a product, and exaggerating those!

- Make it seem as though you are offering something they can't live without!

How do they attract your attention and stick in your memory?

- They can use humour to get you in a good mood;
- They ask questions to hook you in;
- They appeal to your senses;
- They use alliteration, rhyme or a play on words to create a memorable slogan;
- They persuade you to imagine yourself using their product;
- They make you feel special.

Use the following:

- Feel good words

  Attractive   friendly   number one   peaceful
  picturesque   special offer   exciting   once in a
  lifetime   welcoming   happier   slimmer
  healthier   fitter   more intelligent   the envy
  of all your friends   special offer   try now
  genuine   latest fashion   exclusive   look no
  further   guaranteed results   90% of people find
  that ...

- Superlatives

  The best   the tastiest   the bluest   the
  fastest   the prettiest
  the hottest   the comfiest   the friendliest   the
  cheapest   the softest
  only the crumbliest, flakiest chocolate ...

- Imperative (bossy) verbs

  You must ...   explore ...   taste ...   try...   visit ...
  experience ...

  Enjoy ...   delight in ...   discover ...   be amazed
  by ...

- A catchy slogan, perhaps with alliteration. Make it
  big, bold and fun to read so that it really catches
  the reader's attention!

Super, soft sand,   chewy chocolate,   magnificent mountains

- Rhetorical questions – questions that don't need an answer but are used for effect.

Fancy a great holiday break?   Do you want to try the best ... in the world?

Have you ever tried/experienced ...?   Would you like to ...?

How would it feel to ...?   How do you eat yours?

- Organise your advert with bullet points and subheadings

- Use words that STAND OUT!

Persuade   describe   inform   show it's the best

- Use Exaggeration and hyperbole –

The Nation's Favourite,   the best   the most amazing

everyone knows that

Example: New footwear

Are you a Kool Kid?

Only Kool kids ALWAYS wear OKK designer footwear.

- Only Kool Kids can walk for miles!

  Our cushioned sole and shock absorbing heels guarantee a pleasant walk, mile after mile after mile!

- Only Kool kids have cool feet!

  Our trainers have charcoal insoles to absorb sweat and keep you cool and fresh all day long!

- Only Kool Kids have street cred.

  Be the envy of your friends in our stylish trainers

Don't delay! Go out today and buy your own pair of OKK trainers.

The only thing for Kool Kids to be seen in this year!

Example 2: Rainbow Bike

Be the envy of all your friends and ensure you are one of the first to own the brand new fashion statement on wheels - the RAINBOW BIKE

At a special price of only £75.99 until 1st September, this is an offer not to miss - every kid needs one!

Multicoloured, with an amazing cushioned saddle and special, secure safety grip wheels, this new bike is faster than the speed of light and is the perfect tool to get you to school and back each day.

Can you imagine life without it?

Example: Theme Park

Are you tired of having nothing to do at the weekends? Are the kids driving you crazy with theor boredom or demands? Why not head straight to Lost Valley Country Park?

- Meet a range of dinosaurs and extinct animals.
- Excavate the soil to find dinosaur bones.
- Watch a baby dinosaur hatch from its egg.
- Explore our tropical area and feel the gentle tickle as butterflies to settle on your arms.
- Settle down into our wonderful, panoramic restaurant for lunch or for a refreshing cup of tea.

The Lost Valley is actually surprisingly easy to find! Just follow the brown signposts from junction 25 of the M63.

Parking is free and entry is only £10 per person – adult or child!

A great way to turn a dull day into the best day of your holiday!

Persuasive Letters

Be persuasive, not confrontational!

Key Points:

- With a formal letter, start with the name and address of the person you are writing to on the top, left hand side of the paper

- Introduce what you want to say. What are you writing to ask?

- Use flattery!

- Explain your reason

- Give an additional reason

- Generalise – Everyone knows that …

- Use emotions – pull on your reader's heart strings!

- Refer them back to their own childhood or previous experiences

- Exaggerate using WOW words

- Use a rhetorical question to attract the reader's attention

- Try to use alliteration, or a good metaphor or simile

- Use a good conclusory sentence

- Sign off with 'Yours Sincerely' and your name.

Example: Persuasive Letter Requesting a Trip

Mrs Bossy Boots

Greenfield Junior School

Forest Lane

Greentown

Dear Mrs Bossy Boots

I am writing to you because I would like to ask about a possible trip for Y5 to Adventure Island this year.

Everyone agrees that you are the kindest head teacher that this school has ever had and that you do everything in your power to ensure that Greenfield School is an enjoyable place to learn. I am sure that you have noticed that Years 5 and 6 have worked exceptionally hard this year and have produced some outstanding work, particularly in literacy. However, we are all now tired (as are our teachers!) and really need something to give us a boost until the end of term. Everyone knows that a good trip is a great culmination to a hard year's work, and I am sure that you can remember many enjoyable end-of-year trips that you made as a child! For us, we feel that a trip to Adventure Island would be the perfect solution!

In addition, when we returned to school, we would have so much to write about for our next topic, "Theme Parks of England".

I know that if you agreed to this, I would feel as exhilarant as the winner of the lottery! A trip to Adventure Island would be the most sparkling, special and spectacular day of my whole life!

To finish: would you love to give your pupils an extra reward for working so hard this term? Then, if so, please agree to our request. If you were to do so, we would remember it forever!

Thank you very much for reading my letter.

Yours sincerely,

Jamie Smith

Rev & Mrs J M Whoever

The Vicarage

Xtown

Xshire

Dear Mum and Dad

Last night, whilst we were lying in bed, Mary and I could hear you discussing out holiday next year. We would love to be included in this debate and have some suggestions of my own.

As you know, we have been studying French for the last few years of school, and have both always receive good grades in this subject; however, we would love to make them even better! Speaking the language with real. Native speakers is always a good way to develop this.

I also remember, Mum, how you talked about your holidays as a child; and Dad, I recall how you talked about your holidays in France and I wondered – would it be possible for us to stay in a gîte in France somewhere?

I've looked at prices and, compared with our caravan holiday in Northern France last year; the prices are similar. Also, although it is self-catering, Mary and I would be able to help with the food preparation. We would be able to visit the local markets, developing our linguistic abilities at the same time and Thomas could begin to learn some simple words and phrases.

Mary and I really think that this is the best possible option for our summer holiday this year and would love to discuss this with you further

Your loving daughters

Over To You

Now that you're getting the idea of how this genre works, have a go at some of the following.

Warm Up Exercises

- Write a short, catchy slogan to help advertise a new type of:

sweet   car   chocolate bar   bicycle   skateboard
shoe

musical instrument   bed   chair   bin   doll
vacuum cleaner   lamp

clock   TV   pen   bag

Remember:

- You will have to think of a good name for your product.
- Your slogan must be memorable and to the point.

- o You want to make the public feel as though they really need to buy your product!

- Write 5 good reasons why you should be allowed to have Golden Time every Friday.
- Write 5 good, extended reasons why everyone should join in with PE lessons.
- Write some good for and against points to discuss the question 'Mobile phones should be allowed in schools.' Set them up in a table, as below.

For	Against

- Write some good for and against reasons to discuss the question "School uniforms should be banned."
- Write some good for and against reasons for banning homework.

Next, have a go at a few of the following full scale tasks:

Try some full scale adverts: (No illustrations needed – just the phraseology.)

- Write an advert to sell a new chocolate bar.
- Write an advert to sell a new toy or game
- Write an advert to sell a new type of jumper
- Write an advert to sell a new type of footwear
- Write an advert to sell a new type of skateboard or Segway.
- Write an advert to persuade people NOT to do a certain thing!
- Write an advert to sell my business – Heckingbottom Learning!

Try some persuasive letters

- Write a brief letter to persuade your parents to let you have a pet of your choice.
- Write a brief letter to persuade your parents to let you go to a particular place for your holiday this year.
- Write a brief letter persuading your parents to let you celebrate your birthday in a certain way – party, theatre trip, holiday – you choose! Give good reasons.

- Write a brief letter to persuade your teacher (or tutor) to let you off homework this week! (If I'm your tutor, good luck! Very few children win with this one!)

- Write a letter to persuade your parents to buy you a new bike or a new computer.

- Your parents don't want you to have a mobile phone. Write a letter to convince them to get one for you!

- Write a letter to persuade people to eat more bananas, oranges, grapes or other fruits of your choice.

- Write a letter to persuade teachers that children should not have to do homework at weekends.

- Write a letter to persuade your head-teacher that it would be a very good idea to have 'Casual Fridays' every week, when school uniforms do not have to be worn

- Write a letter to the council persuading them that cars should not be allowed in your nearest town over the weekends.

- Someone has written to the local paper complaining about the spiders in their garden. Write a letter to convince them that their fears are wrong

- Someone has written a letter to the national paper saying that the England football team are overpaid.

Write a letter to convince them that they are wrong!

- Write a letter to the Prime Minister suggesting that children should be paid to go to school!

- A suggestion has been made that woodland near you should be cut down and turned into an adventure park. Do you think this is a good idea or not? Write a letter giving your point of view.

Invitations

What is essential to put on an invitation?

- Who is sending the invitation?
- What is the party all about?
- Where is it taking place? Be precise – give detail.
- What times? When does it start? When does it end?
- What is the dress code?
- Who should we reply to?

How detailed can you make your invitation? Can you make it specific to the one person that you are inviting, rather than a vague, general invitation?

Example:

King Stefan and Queen Leah

request the pleasure of the company of

Flora, Fauna and Merryweather

at the baptism of their beloved daughter, the Princess Aurora

in the ballroom of the Royal Palace

on Sunday, 19th June 1216

from 11.30 to 23.30.

Dress code: Formal. Wands may be brought.

RSVP to HRH Queen Leah at The Royal Palace by 1st June

PS - We are hoping that you will feel able to act as Godparents to our lovely daughter.

PPS - Please don't tell Maleficent! Aurora can only have three godmothers and we are nervous as to what she would do if she were to find out that we had not selected her!

Example 2

Celebrate!

Remember! Remember! The 22nd of September.

Come to Frodo and Bilbo's birthday party at Bilbo's dwelling!

Start: 11.00 pm

End; 2:30 am

Come to the best party ever, the best yet;

The party that no-one will ever forget.

Dress: Come dressed in formal clothing.

RSVP to Bilbo

Hope to see you on the night.

Kind regards

Bilbo and Frodo

By Kimon Zannikos (aged 10)

Perfect Your Punctuation Skills

It is impossible to over-emphasise the importance of accurate punctuation in your writing. In the mark scheme I follow, punctuation can score you up to 3 out of 15 points! Add in paragraphing, and you now have a total of 4 points! See what I mean? Other marking schemes that I have seen have shown a similar level of emphasis – showing that it is well worth taking care of.

Basic Punctuation

It is essential to get this right, or it is very likely that you will only get a very low mark for punctuation. Take care – and practise!

Play punctuation detective – finding and correcting errors in pieces of writing helps you to be more aware of where they might be omitted! I do this a lot with my pupils – hidden in many of their comprehensions from the very beginning!

Full Stops and Capital Letters

Capital letters are needed to start new sentences and in proper nouns, such as the names of people and places. They are frequently omitted, even in Years 5 & 6 – but are of vital importance.

One thing that is often overlooked is the word I

Whenever you write the word I – even in a contraction – it needs a capital letter. This includes I've, I'm, I'll, I'd

Over to you:

In your notebook, copy this paragraph, punctuating it correctly with full stops and capital letters

it was a sunny day my mum suggested having a picnic in riverview park we packed up sandwiches fruit and a selection of cakes to take with us when we got to the park we found a nice spot to have our picnic my dad suggested feeding the ducks by the edge of the lake my brother adam thought it would be funny to push me into the lake i was completely drenched when i finally managed to get out i was absolutely furious as id no dry clothes to change into.

Question Marks

As you know, question marks (?) are used to mark a question. As the symbol contains a full stop, the question mark takes its place when a question is being asked.

Don't use the question mark to punctuate an indirect question.

- I wondered what time it was.

- What time is it?

Don't underestimate the power of the question – particularly the rhetorical question – one that doesn't need a specific answer.

What is the role of a rhetorical question?

You're probably answering that for yourself right now. It drags the reader in, making them want to interact with the author, making them think for themselves and making them stand up and take notice of your writing.

Over to you

Rewrite each of the following sentences by changing indirect questions into direct questions.

1. The students asked whether there was any need for more homework.
2. The customer demanded to know why the interest rate was so high.
3. They asked themselves whether they could afford another holiday that year.
4. Molly wondered what the new school build would look like.
5. Jade wanted to know how much the dress was.

Add question marks or full stops to these sentences to show whether they are direct or indirect questions.

1. I wonder if he can help me
2. Can pigs fly
3. She asked how old I was
4. Can I have an extension on my homework
5. I wonder if it is going to be sunny today

Exclamation Marks

These are used to indicate shock and surprise. They follow interjections such as Hey! Wow! They follow short commands such as Stop! Freeze! Go! They indicate astonishment and excitement – and follow the punchline of a joke! Just don't overuse them, or they will lose their effectiveness.

Over to you!

Add an exclamation mark to the following sentences.

1. "Look out" shouted James to his brother.
2. "Ouch" screamed Charlotte.
3. What a wonderful surprise that was
4. "Tidy your room" shouted mother. "It's a pig sty"
5. Looking out at the golden sunset, Maria exclaimed, "This is the life"

Commas

Commas, in their rightful places, are essential.

Look at these two sentences:

- Let's eat, Grandma!

- Let's eat Grandma!

Can you spot the subtle difference between a happy Grandma and a rather worried one?

There's also the well-known description of a panda from the Lynn Truss book.

Panda: Eats, shoots and leaves

That comma turns him into a very dangerous beast indeed!

Panda: Eats shoots and leaves

This is a much tamer, calmer animals!

The top 5 places to use commas are:

1. Splitting sentences into clauses or phrases. Would you benefit from an extra pause as you are reading it? Try a comma!

   After receiving the new that the school holidays were to be extended, jubilant children erupted into the streets.

2. To surround an embedded clause, one that is used to put extra information, in the middle of a sentence

   The boy, who was only three years old, stood on the stairs and yelled for his mother.

   Anna, although only 7, is the best mathematician in the school.

3. Before the F(A)NBOYS conjunctions, but not usually before and!

   For, Nor, But, Or, Yet, So

   You can have the salad, but please don't eat the chips!

   You can have the salad, or you could choose potatoes if you preferred.

   You still haven't eaten your vegetables, so you can't have a fizzy drink!

4. To separate items in a list or lists of adjectives etc.

    She felt tired, depressed and irritated.

    Don't forget to bring pens, pencils, a ruler and an eraser.

5. After many connectives that start a sentence.

    Meanwhile, Jane continued to score full marks in all her tables tests.

    However, it is worth bearing in mind the fact that ...

    Furthermore, it is important to remember the significance ...

Speech Marks

"Speech marks are used around everything that is said," Mum declared. "Any other punctuation will come inside the speech marks."

"Like this question mark?" asked Michael, with a cheeky grin.

"Absolutely," his mother nodded with a smile, "these exclamation marks too!"

"What else do I need to remember if I'm going to punctuate speech correctly?" he queried.

"The new speaker, new line rule is essential. When a different person speaks, you must start a new line."

"Like this?"

"Yes, Michael, like that. Don't forget the comma, name rule when you are addressing people as well!"

"I'll try to remember, Mum!" her son replied.

See the section on writing conversations for more information.

Other Important Punctuation Marks

Beyond the basic punctuation, it's all about 2 main things:

- Using a wide variety of punctuation in the writing

- Using it accurately and in the right way!

<u>Brackets</u> (...)

Brackets are one of the most common ways of adding parenthesis (extra information) to something you are saying – an aside. They can be used to add a short embedded clause or just a couple of words.

Some ways that a parenthesis can be added using brackets include:

1. An extra detail

   The passenger train (which was 5 minutes late) finally pulled up at the station.

   Paul Smith (captain) was praised for his bowling skills.

2. To offer the reader an aside

   I'm heading out (bowling night) but I'll call you back in the morning.

   Amy (my best friend) moved to London last month.

3. To add an authorial intrusion

   Ornithology (what an amazing pass time) kept my cousin thoroughly occupied during his holidays.

4. A list which interrupts a sentence.

Britain's three busiest train stations (Victoria, Kings Cross and St Pancras) are all in London.

5. In biographies, for dates, particularly for the birth and death of a person.

William Tate (February 1798 to April 1873) was the architect who designed Waterloo Bridge Station.

Charles Dickens (1812 – 1870) was the most widely read author of the Victorian era.

Have a go at these in your notebook.

Rewrite the sentences below using brackets:

1. Ellie my older sister lives in Manchester.

2. Jupiter the largest planet is made of gas.

3. The twins Ben and Billy have just played their first football match.

4. The ambulance which had sirens blaring and lights flashing moved swiftly through the traffic.

5. The student who was new to the school got lost to her first lesson.

Rewrite the following paragraph using brackets:

Denver and Max Denver's cousin went to the shopping centre. They had £10 in pound coins between them. Max was hungry. He hadn't eaten all day so he bought a sandwich with halloumi a type of cheese to eat.

<u>Dash</u> –

As we have seen, brackets help you to add extra information; however, whilst the brackets seem to minimise the importance of the words inside, a dash can be used to emphasise the information inside.

Compare these two sentences:

Finally, he was able to return to his normal life (and his Mum)

Finally, he was able to return to his normal life – and his Mum.

A dash does two main jobs, both of which highlight the words that come after – or between them. Use of a dash instead of commas show a higher level awareness of punctuation and may well get you another mark, so it's a skill worth practising. It seems to light that section up, suggesting importance in the overall story and adding depth to your writing.

1. You can use two dashes instead of commas around an embedded clause in a complex sentence.

    Peter – unable to see over the pile of clothes he was carrying – tripped over the pile of rubbish.

    Anna – for the second time that day – fell over her own two feet and landed flat on the floor. When would she learn to walk before she could run?

2. You can replace a single comma with a dash, making the part that follows stand out – giving it greater importance.

   Compare these two sentences.

   Finally, she was going back to her home, to her family, to her Mum

   Finally, she was going back to her home, to her family – to her Mum.

   In the second sentence, the dash signals that it's Mum who is the most important aspect of the return.

In your writing notebook, have a go at some of these:

Copy these sentences. Put in the missing dashes.

1. I'm going to buy chocolates lots of them.
2. When he went to university, his Gran gave him a big pile of money enough to last him a month.
3. The trip has been rescheduled for Monday maybe Thursday.

4. Molly found her purse down the back of the sofa.

5. There is only one meal worth eating pie and chips.

6. Suzi wants to buy Mark a new pair of trainers I can see why.

7. The dog a hairy beast jumped up at me.

8. Permission is granted subject to the following conditions.

9. The films all three of them took years to complete.

Colons :

1. A colon is often used to introduce a list. For example:

   You will need to bring three things to the party: some food; something to drink and a small gift for the host.

2. A colon is also used in a glossary between a word and its definition.

   - *Conjunction: a word used to join two parts of a sentence.*

   - *Adjective: a word which describes a noun.*

   - *Elephant: a large, grey mammal*

3. Finally, the colon can be used to isolate a point for **emphasis** - For example:

   - There's only one word I can use to describe that: fab-u-lous.

   - Remember: never use a comma before 'and' when you are writing a list.

Try these in your writing notebook

Rewrite the sentences below using colons:

　　　1. The colon a useful punctuation mark.

　　　2. My life had changed for ever I was going to university.

　　　3. I can see only one thing the old school building.

　　　4. You have only one choice Leave now while you can.

　　　5. The captive screamed at her captors "You'll never get away with this!"

Colons are used to introduce a list. Put colons in the right places in these sentences:

1. There are seven colours in the rainbow red, orange, yellow, green, blue, indigo and violet.

2. Our remaining opponents for the season are all of the top teams. Manchester United, Liverpool, Chelsea, Arsenal and Newcastle United.

3. My teacher speaks the following languages French, Italian, Spanish and Chinese.

4. I will have three things on my sandwich ham slices, cheese, and mayonnaise.

5. His reasons for wanting a new car were as follows he wanted to be independent, he wanted to stop using public transport and he wanted to impress his girlfriend.

Semi-colons ;

The semi-colon is used to:

1. A semi-colon can sometimes be used to replace a full stop or a connective such as 'and' 'because' or 'but'. It links two complete sentences and turns them into one, each sentence pointing to the other and saying 'Look – we belong!'

   - The door swung open; a masked figure strode in.
   - Mary was weeping with joy; Philip was silent – still in shock
   - He never took any exercise; consequently he became more and more obese.
   - She was very tired; she had worked late the night before.
   - I love writing stories; English has always been my favourite subject
   - I prefer maths to English; it suits my scientific mind better

2. If the items in the list are longer than one or two words, you can separate them with a **semi-colon**. NOTE – you will also use a semi-colon before the 'and' that introduces the last item in the list.

- At the circus we saw: a clown juggling with swords and daggers; a lion who stood on a ball; a fire eater with flashing eyes; and an eight year old acrobat.
- All school children are entitled to the same key things: fun; friendship; fairness; caring adults and teacher; and time to play.

In your writing notebook, have a go with a semi-colon to replace the connectives, commas and even full stops!

1. The rabbit had been sadly neglected and it was in an awful state.
2. John opened the drawer but it was empty.
3. The wedding invitations have all been sent out and two hundred guests are expected.
4. Tom was very clever and worked hard so he deserved to do well in the 11+.
5. Sally's birthday is in November but John's is in September.
6. George ran into the shed because it was raining.
7. Sammy likes hamburgers but I like fish and chips.
8. The car screeched to a halt. The fox managed to escape.
9. Losing money is careless but stealing it is criminal.

Colons or semi-colons – where and why?

1. Mary always tried hard consequently her report was usually outstanding.
2. Colon a punctuation mark consisting of two dots.
3. You will need to bring a sleeping bag a pillow a sheet to go over the plastic mattress and your favourite toy.
4. Remember it is vitally important to bring your wellies!

Colons or semi-colons – where and why? The answer

1. Mary always tried hard; consequently her report was usually outstanding.

    A semi-colon – it's linking 2 sentences

2. Colon: a punctuation mark consisting of two dots.

    Colon – separating out the word from its definition

3. You will need to bring: a sleeping bag; a pillow; a sheet to go over the plastic mattress; and your favourite toy.

4. Colon to introduce the list, semi-colons to separate out all the items – including the last one

5. Remember: it is vitally important to bring your wellies!

    Colon – emphasising the first word.

Writing Themes and Ideas

Here are some themes for writing that you could use. Many of them are used in from earlier in the book, but I'm sure you wouldn't have done all of them straight away – hence they are repeated here for you! I have also added several more in each category – just to keep you going!

Descriptive Writing

 (Remember: It sometimes helps to find a picture on the internet to help you with this!)

Write 6 or 7 well-structured sentences to describe:

- Your favourite animal
- A cat
- A tree in a particular season
- A tree from your imagination
- Your best friend
- A relative of yours that you admire
- A relative or person whom you dislike
- Your ideal bedroom
- Your most precious possession
- Your favourite fruit
- Your favourite meal
- Your favourite food item

- A hot dessert

- A hot desert! (Make sure you know which is which!)

- Your favourite drink

- Your favourite ice-cream

- A vehicle you like (or want to own when you're old enough!)

- Someone's job – be careful to describe!

- An unusual house – there are some lovely ones on Google Images to give you some ideas

- Your favourite place

- A forest

- An orchard

- A flower – from your imagination or one that you can actually see.

- A haunted house

- An alien lands in your garden. Can you describe him?

- Can you describe his spaceship?

- You are standing, facing an unusual door. In 6 or 7 sentences, describe it and describe your feelings as you prepare to open it.

- The door creeks open and you walk in. In 6 or 7 sentences, describe what you can see and how you feel as you walk in.

- You have just walked through a portal into a mysterious new land. In 6 or 7 sentences, describe what is in front of you.
- Imagine you are lost. Write a description to show what you can see and how you feel.

Instructional Writing

In 6 or 7 sentences, give clear instructions as to how to:

- Make cheese/beans/jam on toast
- Make a sandwich
- Make a salad
- Make the most disgusting meal in the world
- Make a fruit smoothie
- Make a glass of orange squash
- Make a refreshing, cold drink
- Make a hot drink of your choice
- Make an ice cream sundae
- Make a birthday card for a friend
- Make a card for a particular festival such as Christmas, Eid, Divali, Channukah

- Bathe a pet

- Wash your hands

- Brush your teeth

- Get dressed for school

- Get an alien/Stone-age child ready for school so they will fit in

- Get changed for PE

- Get ready to go out on a snowy day

- Get ready to go to the beach

- Get ready for a picnic

- Prepare to do some painting

- Draw a dog/cat/elephant etc.

- Make a snowman

- Brush your teeth

- Wash your hands

- Wash your hair

- Clean your shoes

- Put on your socks and shoes

- Play your favourite playground game

- Play your favourite board game

- Play a card game of your choice

- Play a game involving use of dice
- Tidy your bedroom in 5 minutes (think outside the box here!)
- Catch a heffalump or other mysterious creature
- Trap a woolly mammoth
- Feed a dinosaur/dragon/crocodile.
- How to make clouds!

Other Genres

Write 6 or 7 well-constructed sentences for the following:

Diaries

- Write a diary entry for a really great day out/ a horrible day out. Contrasting diary entries are good fun here too!
- Write a diary entry after a school trip
- Write a diary entry for your birthday
- Write a diary entry for your brother/sister's birthday. Think about what you might have been expected to do!
- Write a diary entry from the point of view of an inanimate (non-living) object such as a pencil, a paper

clip, a pen, a toothbrush, a peg, your teddy bear or something you choose for yourself

- Write a diary entry for a soldier in WW1 or WW2
- Write a diary entry for a child who has just been evacuated in WW2
- Imagine you are Charlie Bucket. Write a diary entry for the day you found your golden ticket to Willie Wonka's Chocolate Factory.
- Write a diary entry for a character from one of your reading books
- You have just made an amazing discovery. Write your diary entry.
- You have just invented something mind-shatteringly brilliant. Write your diary entry.
- Write a diary entry for a spy!

Postcards

- Write a postcard from a recent holiday destination
- Write a postcard home in the role of a WW1 soldier from the trenches, or a Roman Soldier in Britain
- Write a postcard home from a child who has just been evacuated in WW2

- Write a postcard after day out for the birthday of one of your siblings!
- Write a postcard from a character in one of your reading books.
- Write a postcard from a family holiday in another country
- Write a postcard from a School Journey (holiday) or other Camp

Conversations and Play scripts

- Write a conversation between you and one of your parents, where you are requesting 10 more minutes before bedtime.
- Write a conversation between you and a friend, where you are arranging to go to the cinema at the weekend.
- Write a conversation between 2 cows in a field
- Write a conversation between 2 goldfish in a bowl.
- Write a conversation between 2 dogs in a park.
- Imagine a tree or a lamp post reacting to a dog who is about to use it as a toilet. Write their conversation.
- Write a conversation between the Wolf and one of the 3 Little Pigs.

- Write a conversation between 2 of the Godmothers of Sleeping Beauty at some stage in the story.

- Write a conversation between an author and one of their characters.

- Turn one of your conversations into a play script (Remember to set the scene and give stage directions!)

- I turned 'Hey Diddle Diddle' into a play script. Take a different Nursery Rhyme and turn it into a play script.

- Write a short scene from a well-known Fairy Tale as a play script. Can you add a twist to it?

- Read a couple of paragraphs of a classic book, particularly a section with dialogue. Can you turn it into a play script?

Persuasive Letters

- Write a brief letter to persuade your parents to let you have a pet of your choice.

- Write a brief letter to persuade your parents to let you go to a particular place for your holiday this year.

- Write a brief letter persuading your parents to let you celebrate your birthday in a certain way – party, theatre trip, holiday – you choose! Give good reasons.

- Write a brief letter to persuade your teacher (or tutor) to let you off homework this week!

Adverts

- Write an advert to sell a new chocolate bar. (No illustrations needed – just the phraseology.)
- Write an advert to sell a new toy or game
- Write an advert to sell a new type of jumper
- Write an advert to sell a new type of footwear
- Write an advert to sell a new type of skateboard or Segway.
- Write an advert to persuade people NOT to do a certain thing!

Invitations

- Write an invitation to a birthday party (NB – have you included all the essential information and have you set it out as an invitation?)
- Write a wedding invitation for Beauty and the Beast
- Write an invitation for Sleeping Beauty's baptism
- Accept an invitation to a party

Ideas for longer writing tasks.

Whilst the Essex 11+ requires you to produce 2 ten-minute pieces of writing, some Entrance exams, especially those for independent schools, may ask for longer pieces – and your teachers certainly will as you prepare for your Year 6 SATs.

Any of the earlier pieces can be extended into longer pieces of writing by adding more detail. You may also like to take some of the ideas I gave you at the beginning of the book for Sentence Openers and take them further. Some of them could make quite gripping stories!

Just so that you don't have to scroll back to the beginning of the book, I have reproduced them here for you!

- o How would you feel if you were to meet a lion? What would you think?
- o What do you think is the most important thing about school? I'll tell you! In my opinion, it is ...
- o Quickly, the boy picked up his book and ran out of the room.
- o Ponderously, the tortoise plodded down the garden, eying the luscious lettuce in the vegetable patch. Would he get there before he was spotted?
- o Running down the hill, she fell over and landed face down in the mud!

- Chasing its tail, the dog looked like a spinning top – or an unlit, spinning Catherine wheel!
- Opening the wrapper carefully, I hear the gentle rustling before the aroma escapes, jumping up to bite me on the nose!
- Squeezing through the tiniest of gaps, she urged herself ever onwards.
- Behind the rock, far away from preying eyes, the tiny mouse sat and waited.
- Near to where the children played, some strange creature was lurking in its lair; something half-human, half-animal. What could it be?
- Although everyone knows that monkeys are mischievous, few people are aware of how naughty they can be.
- Whilst I love all types of fruit, I have to say that by far my favourite is the peach.
- Moreover …
- Nevertheless …
- On the other hand …
- As a result …
- Small, silver and shiny; the coin lay there, unclaimed.
- The umbrella which he held in his arms was, perhaps, the only really normal thing about him.
- The green hat perched precariously on his cheeky, green face made you want to laugh!

- Smaller than all the other fish in the pond, Goldie darted through the weeds.
- More urgent than ever was his need to reach home – to reach his mother.
- The greatest reason has to be …
- Like a somnolent statue perched on his rock, this majestic beast opened his massive mouth to emit an indolent roar.
- Like a silver coin emerging from a black, velvet purse, the moon crept out to brighten the countryside.
- As quiet as a tiny mouse, Emma cautiously emerged from her hiding place. Had he gone? Had he really gone?

What are they looking for in the 11+ tests?

As far as the CSSE is concerned, we have been given no real direction. We know they are marking the exams based on the writing expectations for the old National Curriculum Level 5, but this is all the guidance we have been given!

Below, I have given you the criteria that I use for marking Descriptive writing and Instruction writing in the mock 11+ exams that I run.

Best Fit Scenario	1 mark	2 marks	3 marks
Content	Basic ideas with an introduction & a conclusion. Ideas connected, but not in a way that makes them lively or interesting.	Both pieces of writing are lively & interesting. The content is well developed and interesting. All the ideas are linked through introduction and conclusion	
	Description is appropriate, clear, vivid & interesting	Uses similes and/or metaphors/personification	
	Instructions are appropriate, sequenced, clear & easy to follow.		

Punctuation At least 2 items should be highlighted in any column to score the points in this section.	Demarcates sentences to 95% accuracy with full stops, capital letter & question/ exclamation marks. Uses commas in a list Uses apostrophes for abbreviation	Uses commas to separate subordinate clauses. Uses apostrophes for possession appropriately. Uses 1 from the magic box.	Uses colons & semi-colons appropriately. Uses 2 or more other punctuation marks from the magic box correctly.
	The Magic Box		
	( ) ...	– " " ;	: /

With this are, you can score in areas 1 & 3 without 2 if necessary – and my children often do!

Paragraphs	Sections writing appropriately into 2 or more paragraphs		

Spellin g	Spelling, including that of regular polysyllabic words, is generally accurate.	Writing contains a range of complex, adventurous words, the majority of which are correctly spelt	
Vocabul ary	Uses a range of interesting & challenging vocabulary; however, some challenging word may not be used appropriately	Uses a range of interesting & challenging vocabulary almost always in an appropriate way.	

Senten ce Struct ure	Begins sentences in at least 2 different ways – does not always begin with either the subject or the subject pronoun. Uses at least 2 different connectives	Writing includes a range of complex sentence types. Uses a range of complex connectives, e.g. although, while, whilst, despite, meanwhile and sometimes begins sentences with these. Uses embedded (relative) clauses.	
	Sentence Openers o Start with a question – preferably a rhetorical question. o Start with an adverb or a fronted adverbial – how was the action done? Where did it happen? When did it happen? Silently, the child … o Start with an action – preferably an 'ing' word o Start with a preposition. – Under the table, o Start with a connective - although, because, until etc. o Start with an adjective o Start with the object, rather than the subject		
Total			15

Writing Expectations in years 5 & 6.

Can your child do all this already? How can you encourage them with it?

- I can write sentences in a variety of lengths
- I can use modal verbs e.g. might, should, could, would
- I can use co-ordinating conjunctions (FANBOYS)
- I can use relative clauses (The boy, who had a big head, fell out of the tree.)
- I can use a range of openings such as:
  - Adverbials (some time later, as we ran, once we arrived)
  - Subject reference (they, the boys, our gang)
  - Speech
- I can write different sentence types appropriately e.g:
  - Questions
  - Direct speech
  - Reported speech
  - Commands
- I can use a range of subordinating conjunctions (*whilst, until, despite*) with several subordinate clauses (*Because of their courageous efforts, all of the passengers were saved, which was nothing short*

of a miracle! 'Whilst under my roof, you will obey my rules, which are clearly displayed.)

- I can use subordination at the start of a sentence

- I can use the passive voice *(The centre has been visited often)*

- I can use the subjunctive *(If I were to …, I would …)*

- I can use a range of verb forms *(It will probably leave of its own accord … We could catch a later train, but would we arrive on time?)*

- I can use modifiers e.g. extremely

- I can user a full range of punctuation accurately, including commas to mark phrases and clauses, brackets, dashes, speech marks (inverted commas), ellipsis, colons, semi-colons.

- I can use a range of sentence features to give clarity or emphasis of meaning, including:

  o Fronted adverbials *As a consequence of, Glancing backwards, Some weeks later … etc.*

  o Expanded noun phrases *The mysterious young girl in the portrait*

  o Prepositional phrases *From behind the bike shed. In the event of …*

- I can organise my writing into paragraphs and sections.

- I can make links between topics clear.

- I can make connections between the opening and the ending.

- I can sequence and structure the organization of my paragraphs.

- I can develop information and events in paragraphs and sentences.

- I can prioritise information, write paragraphs chronologically where appropriate, and build tension in paragraphs.

- I can use pronouns (he, she, his, theirs, mine, myself etc.

- I can use adverbials

- I can use subject specific vocabulary

- I can use technical words; vivid language; word choice for effect or emphasis.

- I can make my writing clear and effective and use content to engage and inform the reader

- I can write with features of the appropriate form e.g. appropriate tenses, choice of person, level of formality, correct content and genre, write to the correct audience

- I can write with balanced content

- I can order my writing to engage the reader e.g. placement of significant ideas/event for emphasis; reflective comment; opinion; dialogue.

- I can write with an established and controlled viewpoint with some development of opinion, attitude, position and stance

- I can create appropriate atmosphere in my writing

- I can use vocabulary appropriate to text type

- I can use a range of stylistic features eg:
    - alliteration
    - metaphors
    - puns
    - emotive phrases
    - similes
    - personification

- I can spell most words correctly

- I can use a neat, joined up handwriting style

Further Hints

Make sure you are confident with the basic parts of speech. They come up regularly in comprehension tests. The following websites may help!

http://www.keystage2literacy.co.uk/word-classes.html

http://visuteach.com/free-english-tests

NB you do not need to buy anything here – or even to log in! There are a load of free tests that you can access without logging in, paying or registering, and they are very good for practising!

www.heckingbottomlearning.co.uk

This is my own website and it includes a range of cheap and free booklets to help with 11+ preparation.

Other Books by the same author, also available on Kindle

- 11+ Vocabulary Booster

  A book of activities and flashcards to help to improve your child's vocabulary before they take an 11+ test for a selective school (UK). This book includes more than 1000 11+ type vocabulary questions.

  It is also useful for anyone learning English, or preparing for any major exam towards the end of Primary education.

  A sample from this book is enclosed on the next few pages.

- A Quick Guide to Figurative Language

  In today's increasingly competitive society, preparation for the 11+ has become incredibly tough, whichever education authority area you live in. For your child, it involves studying many concepts that they will not have faced before. Many of the questions are extremely hard, and not all the elements of the exam can be fully prepared for; however, even in the areas of the country where they now claim the exams cannot be 'tutored', there are still many tools that you can give your children to help their preparation - and one of those tools is a knowledge of the different aspects of Figurative Language.

Introducing metaphors and similes, personification and pathetic fallacy, alliteration, idioms, onomatopoeia, hyperbole and oxymoron in a way that they will be easily remembered, this book is a great introduction to Figurative Language for children from Upper Key Stage 2 to the end of Key Stage 3 (9 to 14 year olds)

- **Richard's Magic Book**

Richard is an 8 1/2 year old boy who, like many boys of his age, simply hates reading. He views it as a waste of time - after all, there are plenty of other things that he could be doing ... such as watching TV, playing on the WII or on his Nintendo. But all this changes when his teacher gives him a special book. As he says 'I had to give it to you. It has your name on the cover!' And it does. It's called 'Richard's Magic Book'. Reluctantly, Richard takes it home to read ... and is astounded to find that it really IS all about him!

Before long, he meets a small elf called Nilbog who takes him on a series of magic adventures. The only catch is that, for the magic to work, he has to keep reading the book; however, the good side to this is that the book continues to be all about him and about his magical adventures.

His adventures take him to the North Pole, where he meets Ralop, the Polar Bear; under the sea, where he meets the Merpeople and Krash, the shark; to Fantasy Land where he meets Nicornu; into his garden where he meets the ants and finally to an encounter with a giant called Ergo.

- Richards Magical Day Out – (coming soon)

  A sequel to Richard's Magic Book.

  Richard's father takes him sea fishing – he's feeling well and truly fed up, as he could think of many other, better things to do on a day out ... until, that is, Nilbog appears and he goes on another adventure with old friends.

- Can We Play Maths Again Today, Please?

  Build Your Child's Confidence in Mathematics through Games and Activities – A Guide for Parents and other key carers.

  Three sample chapters, especially chosen for 11+ candidates, have been enclosed in the following pages of this book.

- Are We Nearly there Yet?

A book packed with a range games and activities to play in the car – both on long journeys and on short journeys, such as the School Run.

- Fantastical Facts for Quizzical Kids

  A book of amazing facts, quizzes and trivia to amaze and interest children who have a lively and healthy interest in the world around them.
  This is also a great book to boost the General Knowledge of a child who is about to tackle the 11+

11+ Vocabulary Booster – Sample pages

<u>Synonyms</u> are words which are very close in meaning to one another – such as open and ajar; hide and conceal; sleep and doze.

<u>Antonyms</u> are words that are OPPOSITE in meaning to one another – such as open and closed, reveal and conceal, awake and asleep.

Look at the groups of words below and select the **TWO SYNONYMS** (words which are closest in meaning) - one from each set.

a. (perfect, cradle, moon)   (sunshine, baby, faultless)

b. (splash, scrape, new)   (flash, flesh, fresh)

c. (inside, extent, incense) (outside, interior, outdoors)

d. (thunder, snowstorm, hail)   (sleet, blizzard, lightning)

e. (different, similar, odd) (alike, even, quiet)

f. (cease, crease, wrinkle) (stop, start, iron)

g. (solution, excuse, remedy)   (lie, tell, reason)

h. (amaze, astound, maze)   (fun, garden, labyrinth)

i. (drink, drank, drunk)   (water, juice, intoxicated)

The answers!

a. (<u>perfect,</u> cradle, moon) (sunshine, baby, <u>faultless</u>)

b. (splash, scrape, <u>new</u>) (flash, flesh, <u>fresh</u>)

c. (<u>inside,</u> extent, incense) (outside, <u>interior,</u> outdoors)

d. (thunder, <u>snowstorm,</u> hail) (sleet, <u>blizzard,</u> lightning)

e. (different, <u>similar,</u> odd) (<u>alike,</u> even, quiet)

f. (<u>cease,</u> crease, wrinkle) (<u>stop,</u> start, iron)

g. (solution, <u>excuse,</u> remedy) (lie, tell, <u>reason</u>)

h. (amaze, astound, <u>maze</u>) (fun, garden, <u>labyrinth</u>)

i. (drink, drank, <u>drunk</u>) (water, juice, <u>intoxicated</u>)

Notes

- The opposite of interior is exterior!
- Whilst hail and sleet are relatively similar in that they are both forms of cold precipitation, snowstorm and blizzard are virtually the same
- Drink, drank, drunk is always a funny one, especially when you look at the way the tenses work. John drinks the wine, John drank the wine; the wine was drunk (and so was John – he was intoxicated!)

Look at the groups of words below and select the **TWO** antonyms (words which are most opposite in meaning) – one from each group.

(hour, small, huge)   (minute, clock, chair)

(loud, expensive, gentle) (dear, quiet, noise)

(rear, fear, near)   (back, tear, far)

(inside, insect, incapable) (capable, side, sect)

(swim, float, dive)   (bath, sink, toilet)

(dear, sweetheart, love) (nice, cheap, expensive)

(few, minority many)   (mostly majority certainly)

(glib timid tiresome)   (fib bold blame)

(foolish ignoramus rude) (wise known discourteous)

The Answers!

(hour, small, <u>huge</u>)   (<u>minute</u>, clock, chair)

(<u>loud</u>, expensive, gentle) (dear, <u>quiet</u>, noise)

(rear, fear, <u>near</u>)   (back, tear, <u>far</u>)

(inside, insect, <u>incapable</u>) (<u>capable</u>, side, sect)

(swim, <u>float</u>, dive)   (bath, <u>sink</u>, toilet)

(<u>dear</u>, sweetheart, love) (nice, <u>cheap</u>, expensive)

(few, <u>minority</u> many)   (mostly <u>majority</u> certainly)

(glib <u>timid</u> tiresome)   (fib <u>bold</u> blame)

(<u>foolish</u> ignoramus rude) (<u>wise</u> known discourteous)

The first pair of words on this page causes problems for a great many people, who try to match hour and minute as opposites. Far from being opposites, these are merely different periods of time.

Minute is a homonym. There are two very different ways of pronouncing the word, each of which has a totally different meaning, as in the sentence:

A <u>minute</u> is a <u>minute</u> period of time

- In the first use of the word, it is pronounced 'min-it' and it is a short period of time

- The second time I used the word in the sentence above, you need to pronounce it as 'my-newt' and you have a synonym for miniscule or tiny.

<u>Joke Time!</u>
    Although he is not particularly small, I call my pet amphibian 'Tiny' because he is <u>my newt</u>!

To find out more, go to www.amazon.co.uk and download the 11+ Vocabulary Booster

http://www.amazon.co.uk/11-Vocabulary-Booster-Support-ebook/dp/B00CEOUOT2/ref=sr_1_2?ie=UTF8&qid=1375667149&sr=8-2&keywords=11%2B+vocabulary

A Quick Guide to Figurative Language - sample pages.

Metaphors and Similes

Metaphors and similes are very closely related; in fact the same description can often be used in both formats.

Quite basically, a metaphor IS, whereas a simile is LIKE.

Look at these examples to help you.

His room is a pigsty (metaphor)

His room is like a pigsty (simile)

His room is as messy as a pigsty (simile)

His room is similar to a pigsty (simile)

Metaphors

A metaphor says that something actually IS something totally different – something that it could not possibly be.

Here are some examples:

- The moon is a silver coin hiding in a black velvet purse
- A blanket of snow covered the ground
- The test was a walk in the park
- Words are the weapons with which we wound those around us.

How many more can you think of?

Similes

A simile relates to similarities, i.e. saying that something is LIKE, AS or SIMILAR TO something else.

Here are some examples:

- She was as quiet as a mouse
- The room looked like a bomb had hit it
- You eat like a horse
- She sleeps like a baby
- She is as stubborn as a mule
- The children's eyes gleamed like pearls.
- The pirate's eyes were as black as coal.

Look at these sets of metaphors and similes taken from a book by an author, Cynthia Harrod Eagles, who writes for adults. These descriptions come from a section describing a funeral.

'The church was a cave full of jewels – a treasure trove, filled with winking diamond points of light.'

- Is this a metaphor or a simile?
- What is the key word that shows you this?
- Now close your eyes and try to picture this.

  Is it an effective description?

  In what way?

'The altar was so weighted with candles; it looked like a fire-ship'

Fire ships were used in the days of wooden ships and were ships filled with flammable objects which were then deliberately set on fire and were either steered or allowed to drift into an enemy fleet, in order to destroy ships, or to create panic and make the enemy break formation.

- Is this a metaphor or a simile?
- What is the key word that shows you this?
- Now close your eyes and try to picture this.

  Is it an effective description?

  In what way?

Now look at this phrase adapted from another book by the same author:

'The caretaker lived like a crab in a dark cave by the front door and only scuttled out to sweep the entrance.'

<u>Simile:</u> The caretaker lived *like a crab*

Notice the way he is later described as having 'scuttled', which enhances the simile further.

- What is the key word that shows you that this is a simile?
- Now close your eyes and try to picture this.
- Is it an effective description? In what way?

<u>Metaphor:</u> *lived ... in a dark cave by the front door.*

Clearly, he did not actually live in a dark cave ... he must have lived in a room.

What does the use of the word 'cave' tell you about the room he lived in?

Try to draw the caretaker and his room from the little information that you have been given. Do you find it effective?

Over to You

Metaphors are trickier than similes, because you have to be very careful not to use words such as 'like' or 'as'. You have to say that something IS something different.

E.g. My little sister is a monkey; Our classroom is a zoo.

1. The teacher said 'James is a clown'. What did she mean by that?

2. Mum said 'Maria is such an angel'. What do you think she meant?

3. What metaphor could you write for someone who is a very fast runner?

4. What metaphor could you use to describe a very clever person?

5. What metaphor could you use to describe the blossom on a tree?

6. What metaphor could you use to describe your teacher?

7. Can you think of a metaphor to describe your pet or another animal?

8. Can you think of a metaphor to describe the sun?

For more information, look at this book on Amazon

https://www.amazon.co.uk/Quick-Guide-Figurative-Language-Support-ebook/dp/B00ED40GMG/ref=sr_1_2?s=digital-text&ie=UTF8&qid=1466378283&sr=1-2&keywords=figurative+language

Can We Play Maths Today, Please?

Here are three sample chapters which have been adapted from the book to suit trainee 11+ candidates, one of which look at activities with dice, one which looks at activities with playing cards, and one additional chapter which introduces the concept of BIDMAS, which is essential for tackling the 11+ maths papers.

Using Dice

There are a great many games and activities that merely involve use of dice; not just board games and Yahtzee! Obviously, the more dice you use, the more complicated the games are; but the options are virtually limitless.

Two Dice

- Roll two dice and work out the product of the two numbers. Who can score the greatest total?

Three Dice

- Roll three dice and work out the sum of all three. Who can score the largest total?

- Roll two dice and work out their sum to give you your first number. Roll the third die and calculate the product of your two numbers. Who can score the greatest total?

What is the highest possible total? How can you work it out?

- Roll three dice and work out the product of the three numbers rolled. Who can score the highest product? (This includes looking at cubed numbers to 6 cubed – which can be tricky, but which often occur on the maths papers)

Four Dice

- Roll four dice and work out the sum of all four. Who can score the largest total?

- Roll two dice and work out their sum to give you your first number. Next, roll the other two and work out their sum to give you your second number. Work out the product of the two numbers. Who can score the greatest total?

- Roll 4 dice; use addition and multiplication to work out the highest possible answer that can be made from your combination of numbers

- Roll all four dice. How many different totals can you make with your four dice in five minutes? Can you use some of the rules of BIDMAS (explained later) to help you?

e.g. you roll…

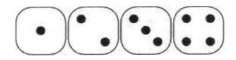

You could score…

1 + 2 + 3 + 4 = 10

1 x 2 x 3 x 4 = 24

(1 + 2) x (3 + 4) = 21

(1 + 2) x 3 x 4 = 36

etc.

Score 1 point for every different total made. Score 20 points to gain a 'reward'.

Year 6 children can use aspects of BIDMAS in their answers, in which case, they may like to check their answers on a scientific calculator.

Six Dice

- Roll all six dice and work out the total sum. Who can score the largest total?

- Roll two dice and work out their sum to give you your first number and multiply it by one of the others. Choose the three of your dice that will give the greatest product and declare it. Who can score the greatest total?

  How many different totals can your child make in 5 minutes?

- Choose 3 of your dice and work out their product. Who can score the highest product?

- Mega tricky game! Roll all six dice. How many different totals can you make with your six dice in five minutes?

e.g. you roll...

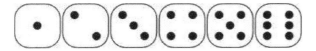

You could score...

1 + 2 + 3 + 4 + 5 + 6 = 21

1 x 2 x 3 x 4 x 5 x 6 = 720

(1 + 2) x (3 + 4) x (5 + 6) = 21 x 11 = 231

Or you could use just a few of your dice

1 + 2 + 3 + 4 = 10

1 x 2 x 3 x 4 = 24

(1 + 2) x (3 + 4) = 21

(1 + 2) x 3 x 4 = 36

etc.

Score 1 point for every different total made and 2 points for the highest total each time. Score 20 points to gain a 'reward'.

11+ candidates and Year 6 children can use aspects of BIDMAS in their answers, in which case, they may like to check their answers on a scientific calculator.

Using Polyhedral Dice

A range of different polyhedral dice can be purchased online, both through Amazon and also through eBay. Use of these widen the range of numbers usable in games and raise the limits infinitely.

Put a set of these down in front of you child from around Years 3/4 after having played a range of dice games and step back. See what they can come up with! Children can be quite ingenious with their ideas; particularly after having been challenged by use of unusual tools!

Using Playing Cards

There are literally hundreds of games that can be played using an ordinary pack of playing games. From simple number matching games such as 'snap' to games which involve more complex mathematical skills, the options are virtually limitless. Many ideas have been included in the year group sections of this book; however, here are a few others that you might like to try.

Snap

Everyone knows this game! Divide the cards equally between the players; then take it in turns to place a card on the pile. When the two top cards match, the first player to shout 'snap' takes the pile. The winner is the player with the most cards at the end of game.

Thirteen

Like 'snap' but this time you shout when the top two cards total 13. In this game, an ace counts as 1, jack as 11, queen as 12 and king as 13 (so wins as a solo card!)

Twenty Four

As above, but this time looking at the product of the top two cards. When the product is 24, shout out!

Because 24 is a number that has a lot of factors, it is a fairly easy total to work towards; however, you might like to change the challenge to other numbers. Any multiple of 12 is good – 36 is very good!

Deal 'em - Adders.

This activity is great for rapid addition work and number bond revision.

Remove all the 'royal' cards from the pack, leaving you with a standard pack of ace to ten cards in the four suits. Shuffle the cards thoroughly and place them face down on the table. Take it in turns to turn over the top card, adding its total to the ones already turned.

e.g. You turn over the 5

Your child turns over the 7 and shouts out '12'

You turn over a 6 – your child shouts '18'

Your child turns over a 3 – '21' etc.

Deal 'em – Subtractors.

Play as above, but subtract from 110

e.g. You turn over the 5. Your child shouts out '105'

Your child turns over the 7 and shouts out '98'

You turn over a 6 – your child shouts '92'

Your child turns over a 3 – '89' etc.

Deal 'em Positive and negative

This is a game for children from the top of Year 4 into years 5 and 6

Just like the previous games, remove the 'royal' cards from your hand first, then shuffle the cards and place them in a pile in the centre of the table. Turn them over, one at a time. In this version of the game, however, black cards are 'positive' – so you add those. Red cards are negative – so their scores are subtracted from the total.

If played correctly, your final total should be 0; although you should pass through a range of negative numbers in the process.

Once your child gets good at this, you might like to 'fiddle' the shuffle to ensure that 3 or 4 red cards are encountered in a row, ensuring the use if negative totals – if you think you can get away with a bit of simple cheating!

Jubilee

A game for between 2 & 8 players (although for more than 4 players, I recommend the use of 2 packs of cards).

Starting with a full set of cards, shuffle them carefully and place them in the centre of the table.

One player turns over the cards, mentally adding each number to the previous total until a Royal card (Jack, Queen or King) is turned – at which point, the opponents shout 'Jubilee'. Their score is frozen and written down before the turn is passed to the next player.

If they get another go, they continue from their previous total.

The winner is the one who has reached the highest total once the last card has been turned.

Variations on this Game

Whilst at the earlier stages, you might like to shout 'Jubilee' for every Royal card; once your child becomes more confident, you may want to save this purely for Kings.

Jubilee Plus & Jubilee Minus.

Starting with a full set of cards, shuffle them carefully and place them in the centre of the table.

In this version of the game, red cards are all negative; whereas black cards are always positive.

One player turns over the cards, adding or subtracting each number to/from the previous total until a Royal card is turned – at which point, the opponents shout 'Jubilee'. Their score is frozen and written down before the turn is passed to the next player.

If they get another go, they continue from their previous total.

The winner is the one who has reached the highest total once the last card has been turned.

Variation on this Game

Whilst at the earlier stages, you might like to shout 'Jubilee' for every Royal card; once your child becomes more confident, you may want to save this purely for Kings, which results in speedier play.

Deal 'em Tables.

Take a pack of cards and remove all the 'Royals'. Shuffle well and place upside down on the table. Take it in turns to turn over the top card and multiply it to the one previously on top, calling out the product of the two.

e.g. You turn over the 5

Your child turns over a 7 and calls out ' 5 × 7 = 35'

You turn over a 4 – '7 × 4 = 28'

Your child turns over an 8 – '4 × 8 = 32'

You turn over a 6 – '6 x 8 = 48'

Etc.

If your child is good at this, introduce the 'Royals' so that a jack is 11, a Queen is 12 and a King is 13; then play as above.

To make it really hard, try making the red cards negative numbers and the black cards positive. What do they do when they turn 2 red cards over? What happens with a red card and a black one? Is it always the same?

Twenty-one

This is a simplified version of the casino game, without the gambling involved. Deal 2 cards to your child and two to yourself. They look at their cards and add up the total, deciding whether any Ace in their hand counts as a 1 or 11. All other 'royal' cards count as 10. They then decide whether to stick (keep their current total) or twist (risk taking another card). You then turn your cards over. The player whose total is nearest to, but not exceeding, 21 is the winner and scores a point. Anyone who has scored exactly 21 scores 2 points. Score 3 points if you have manages it in 2 cards. Set a target number of points for the end of the match and stick to it.

<u>Regal Twenty-one</u>

Make '21' more complex by counting the 'Royal' cards as: jack = 11; Queen = 12; King = 13. Score as above.

BIDMAS

As you will have noticed from the sections above, by Years 5 & 6, your child will be moving on to some quite difficult aspects of maths; one of the trickiest of which is BIDMAS (sometimes also referred to as BODMAS). This is a concept that often catches parents out, as well as children. Frequently, I have parents ask me why the answer to a question is wrong, and then I find myself having to explain BIDMAS to them as well!

Here is a brief explanation of what BIDMAS is all about for those of you who are unsure.

First of all, however, try this sum

$$4 + 6 \times 8 =$$

If you said 52; well done! You clearly already know what BIDMAS is. If, however, your response was 80 and you can't see where I got my answer of 52 from; don't worry.

You are not alone, but you will need to read the explanation below!

This type of problem catches a lot of people out, and a normal calculator will also give you the faulty answer of 80 for this particular question. The reason is that it is incapable of sorting the whole sum and so dealing the relative parts of the problem in the correct order. If you try the same sum on a scientific calculator, you will see that it believes that the answer should be 52, because it doesn't solve the problem as you input each section and so is able to apply the rules of BIDMAS; which state the order of any calculation should be:

- Brackets – these should always be solved first, wherever they might appear in the sum

- Indices or Powers Of – e.g. 5^2. These should be solved next, regardless of where they appear in the sum.

- Division & Multiplication. These are solved next; but this time, they are solved in the order that they appear in the sum.

- Addition & Subtraction. When only addition and subtraction are left, start from the left hand side and work through them in the order in which they appear in the sum.

In other words, you should always multiply BEFORE adding; even if the addition looks to come first in the sum.

6 x 8 = 48 + 4 = 52. (An answer of 80 is usually described as being a BADMIS in my class, for more reasons than one!)

Example 2

What is 4 + 5 x 3?

In BIDMAS, multiplication comes before addition, so multiply 5 by 3 first.

4 + 5 × 3 = 4 + 15 = 19, so this is the right answer.

(27 is a BADMIS – you have added before multiplying.)

To find this book on Amazon, go to
https://www.amazon.co.uk/Maths-Today-Please-Educational-games-ebook/dp/B0085P7UKU/ref=sr_1_1?s=digital-text&ie=UTF8&qid=1466378469&sr=1-1&keywords=can+we+play+maths

16006237R00100

Printed in Great Britain
by Amazon